MARCUS
EVERYDAY

HarperCollins*Publishers*
1 London Bridge Street
London SE1 9GF

www.harpercollins.co.uk

First published by HarperCollins*Publishers* 2019

10 9 8 7 6 5 4 3 2 1

A catalogue record of this book is available from the
British Library.

ISBN 978-0-00-832099-7

Food styling: Becks Wilkinson
Prop styling: Tabitha Hawkins

Printed and bound by GPS Group

MIX
**Paper from
responsible sources**
FSC
www.fsc.org **FSC™ C007454**

FSC™ is a non-profit international organisation established to promote the
responsible management of the world's forests. Products carrying the FSC
label are independently certified to assure consumers that they come from
forests that are managed to meet the social, economic and ecological needs
of present and future generations, and other controlled sources.

Find out more about HarperCollins and the environment at
www.harpercollins.co.uk/green

COOK'S NOTES

Unless otherwise stated:

Use medium free-range eggs

Use whole milk (but semi-skimmed
can be substituted, if you like)

Use unsalted butter

Use standard plain flour

Use medium-sized fruit and vegetables

Use medium-sized meat and fish portions.
(A medium-sized fish portion is 170–180g and
a medium-sized meat portion is 200–220g.)

Always allow meat and fish to come to room
temperature before you cook them. They
shouldn't be cooked fridge-cold.

Use fresh herbs – 1 bunch = 25g

MARCUS EVERYDAY

MARCUS WAREING

WITH CHANTELLE NICHOLSON

PHOTOGRAPHY BY
SUSAN BELL

 HarperCollins*Publishers*

Introduction

Everyday cookery should be just that: something that is achievable on a daily basis and fits in with the busy lives we all lead. This book of recipes for great home cookery will enable anyone to create something delicious and exciting for the whole family, for every occasion.

Each chapter has earned its place in this book and came to mind when I started thinking about how I live my life and how I view food when I'm not being a chef and am in my kitchen at home. It's about my life outside my work, but the inspiration still comes from being a chef – the two are intertwined. This book is divided into eight chapters, which, from my perspective, cover all the different demands and challenges of everyday cookery and provide a resource for absolutely anyone to create something wonderful in their kitchen. I wanted to explore everything from easy weeknight dinners to ideas for what to eat on holidays, and anything in between.

Home cookery is, and always will be, a way of creating many positive connections through food; from knowing what is in the food on your plate, to minimising what you waste and to the sense of enjoyment gained by knowing that you've created something delicious with your own hands.

In the autumn of 2017 I acquired a property in East Sussex called Melfort House, which has given us an opportunity to spend quality time together as a family all year round, away from the hustle and bustle of London. One of the big pluses for me was the farm and arable land that came with the house: there was an overgrown and unused kitchen garden, a small orchard, some beehives and huge potential for more in terms of what they could produce.

For me, 2018 was a year of discovery. What would grow? Where, and how? What would the yield be? After a huge clearout and clean up, small green shoots were celebrated with a sense of anticipation of what they would grow into. Even though I've been a chef for more than 30 years, this has been the one part of the process I hadn't yet experienced; the growing and harvesting of the produce.

I feel like a child again when I'm there, and the kitchen garden, the bees, the orchard, the apples, the pears … they all inspire me as a chef. We transported numerous boxes of freshly harvested fruit and vegetables, as well as honey from the beehives, in the back of the car into central London, to the chefs in my kitchens. Their excitement was a joy to see. The logistical challenge of growing, harvesting and then getting produce from Sussex to London was a little trial and error, and we learned a lot in the first year. I'm currently creating a pond at the back of the house, around which we're growing herbs and wild flowers to use in the restaurant. But I have even bigger plans, so watch this space!

I have therefore dedicated a whole chapter to celebrating my first year at Melfort – 'My Garden Patch'. While you may not have your own garden patch, you can source some great produce from farmers' markets, community gardens, and even your local supermarket. Or sign up for online vegetable boxes. We sometimes forget to celebrate the humble vegetable, instead spending time sourcing and investing in a great joint of beef or other meat. I implore you to put the same effort into sourcing good-quality garden produce and use this chapter to inspire you. My kids now know the difference in taste between tomatoes grown under the sun, harvested within their rightful season, and the tomatoes from the supermarket – they're chalk and cheese! But what I've also taught them is how to take those everyday tomatoes we all buy and improve their flavour if we need to.

What you will also see scattered throughout the book is a focus on honey as a fantastic ingredient, used in many different ways. Having comb honey from our own bees at Melfort has made me think about this ingredient in a completely different way and about the flowers (in particular the lavender and roses) they pollinate – all of which flavour our honey. This ingredient that I have always taken for granted as a cook suddenly has magical implications now that I've witnessed its making.

Running a restaurant kitchen from a young age instilled in me an awareness of waste and resourcefulness; of not wanting to needlessly discard a single thing. The cost of food, how you prepare it and how you eventually sell it, can make or break a restaurant business. The notion of throwing something in the bin that could still be used is sacrilege to me. So, for me, this principle should also be applied at home. After *Marcus at Home* and *New Classics* I wanted to write a book that celebrated home cookery and seasonal produce, which would also be a practical guide to creating delicious meals from ingredients that may not have been completely used up, or might otherwise typically be destined for the bin.

We are bombarded with a constant stream of news about environmental issues. The sheer amount of food that we, as a nation, waste on a daily basis is a huge problem. Food gets stacked up in the fridge, then we overbuy – throwing things into our shopping baskets because we think we need it, without necessarily looking in the fridge before we go shopping and planning what we're buying for. It's so easy to buy more than we need, be seduced by 2-for-1 deals and so on. We need to start buying only what we're actually going to eat. Things go off, of course, but having been taught as a young man by my father to appreciate fresh produce, I know how not to take an ingredient for granted as well as how to use it up resourcefully.

The chapter 'Waste Not, Want Not' came about originally because of the sheer volume of some of the Melfort produce (tomatoes, for example) that I could not keep up with, and the recipes that I used to avoid throwing anything away. This chapter provides a framework for how to use what you may have a glut of, but also how to breathe new life into that old potato lying at the bottom of your pantry, or that slightly shrivelled orange in your fruit bowl.

I also felt there was a need for a chapter on cooking solo – 'Home Alone'. Instead of having a cheese sandwich, or ordering a takeout, try these recipes to give yourself a bit of a treat (my favourite is the Sirloin Steak with Brandy Sauce and Crispy Potatoes on page 130), and enjoy the silence.

I've included handy methods and tips throughout the book for how to cook ingredients the way that I, as a chef, cook them. It's intuitive for me, but I have realised when cooking at home with my family and friends that there are certain techniques and procedures that transform a dish from being just okay to being great, such as how to cook a steak, how to make perfect mashed potato, and my foolproof method for cooking omelettes. As well as what to do when things don't quite go to plan ...

Everyone thinks chefs make everything from scratch when they cook at home, but I don't. Like so many, my life doesn't allow me to do that. Instead, I take basic things, like an average shop-bought mayonnaise, which can be a little bland, and make it better. I'll enhance it with garlic, or curry seasoning, or a little bit of saffron or herbs – anything, really. Even gherkins or chillies – it's easy to improve it. I also use stock cubes like salt, as a seasoning, crumbling one over a dish as a flavour enhancer. I still wouldn't ever mess with baked beans, though (apart from maybe adding a bit of HP Sauce).

I've been a cook since I was 14 years old, and ran restaurants as a head chef from the age of 25, so much of my life has been spent in a professional kitchen. This book is about a different style of cooking, and is about me in my everyday life. Some of the recipes will look familiar, but there are little twists, anecdotes, secrets and tips. These are the things that make chefs seem different to everybody else – it might appear that we have a Midas touch, but it's really just layer upon layer of training.

I hope you enjoy cooking the recipes as much as I enjoyed writing them. As I've gone through the process of writing cookbooks, I've been fascinated by the journey; moving forward, rethinking, recreating and reinventing new ideas, which is what I do in my professional kitchen. I want this book to be used by everyone, every single day. Spending your time in the kitchen creatively is an integral part of the process of preparing good food – it's not just about the delicious end result. And these recipes are perfect for that.

Roasted and Pickled Cauliflower Salad with Almonds and Chives

Beetroot, Tahini Verde and Sourdough Salad

Crispy Courgettes with Goats' Cheese and Lavender Honey

Tomato, Wild Garlic and Burrata Salad

Chilled Summer Garden Soup with Lemon and Mackerel

Asparagus with Bagna Cáuda and Parmesan

Roasted Jerusalem Artichokes with Prunes, Lentils and Sour Cream

Carrots with Pine Nuts and Tarragon

Parsnip, Rosemary and Horseradish Gratin

Celeriac, Ham Hock and Barley Hot Pot

Poached Rhubarb and Rhubarb Jelly with Bay Leaf Cream and Shortbread

Strawberry and Mint Eton Mess

Gooseberry and Basil Fool

Caramelised Honey-roasted Pears with Mascarpone and Filo

Harvest Preservation
Fermenting – Fennel Kimchi
Pickling – Pickled Cucumbers
Jam-making – Fig Jam
Chutney Making – Apple, Rhubarb and Rosemary Chutney

My Garden Patch

My Garden Patch

This chapter is all about my new life at Melfort House. I feel like a young boy when I'm there. I'm finding a new sense of understanding and energy from ingredients I've never used much before – until now my life has always been about professional kitchens. The photographs in this chapter are also special to me – they were taken at the start of the photoshoot, capturing not just the end of summer but the beginning of this book. We were so blessed on that day, with the sunshine and everything jumping out of the ground; we were pulling up beetroots and cabbages, herbs and celery; it was magical. Just don't ask me to choose a favourite dish in this chapter, because I can't!

Beetroot, Tahini Verde and Sourdough Salad

SERVES: 4 | PREP TIME: ABOUT 25 MINUTES | COOKING TIME: ABOUT 1 HOUR, PLUS COOLING

Beetroot is so versatile, and it grows very easily. I plant a few different varieties, which gives a great variation of sweetness and colour. Tahini verde is a sesame sauce full of garden herbs. It adds a burst of freshness, flavour and richness to the dish. It will keep for a couple of days in the fridge and is wonderful for salads and with fish. If you can't find beetroot with leaves intact, use 50g salad leaves instead.

8 large red beetroots, leaves removed, washed and set aside
50ml red wine vinegar, plus 1 tbsp
2 bay leaves
5 cloves
1 tbsp table salt
6 tbsp olive oil
2 candy beetroots, peeled
4 slices of sourdough (about 200g)
sea salt and freshly ground black pepper

FOR THE TAHINI VERDE
100g tahini
2 tbsp chopped tarragon leaves
2 tbsp chopped coriander leaves
2 tbsp chopped mint leaves
2 tbsp chopped basil leaves
½ tsp table salt

1. Put the red beetroots in a saucepan and cover with water. Add the 50ml of red wine vinegar, bay leaves, cloves and the salt. Bring to the boil and cook for about 1 hour, or until just tender. Remove from the heat, drain, leave to cool, then peel and cut each one into 4–6 wedges. Put them in a bowl, drizzle with 1 tablespoon of the olive oil and season with salt and pepper. Set aside.

2. Cut the peeled candy beetroots into 1–2mm-thick rounds, using a mandoline if you have one. Set aside.

3. To make the tahini verde, place all of the ingredients in the bowl of a small food processor, or a beaker for a stick blender, add 50ml cold water and blitz together to form a slightly chunky dressing.

4. Mix 3 tablespoons of the olive oil with the tablespoon of red wine vinegar in a bowl to form a vinaigrette, then set aside.

5. Brush the sourdough with the remaining olive oil and break it into chunky croutons. Season with salt and pepper. Heat a large frying pan over high heat, add the croutons and toast for 3–5 minutes.

6. Dress the beetroot leaves and candy beetroot slices with the vinaigrette.

7. Place the cooked beetroot wedges, dressed leaves and raw candy beetroot slices on a serving dish with the sourdough croutons. Dollop the tahini verde on top and serve.

MARCUS' TIP:
I use a lot of bay leaves in my cooking, though they have a pungent flavour so one goes a long way. Plant a bay tree (in the garden or in a pot) – they are very hardy and do not take up much space. This will give you everyday access to the leaves.

Roasted and Pickled Cauliflower Salad with Almonds and Chives

SERVES: 4 | PREP TIME: 20 MINUTES | COOKING TIME: 30 MINUTES

One of the most versatile vegetables around, the humble cauliflower is also a hardy plant (as well as being very attractive to caterpillars, we've found). I like the combination of the nutty, roasted cauliflower in this dish with the sour zing of the pickled cauliflower, which you can prepare up to 12 hours ahead. The toasted almonds also add a richness to the dish and the chives bring a refreshing oniony hit.

2 heads of cauliflower, leaves removed
60g butter, cubed
½ bunch of chives, cut in half
sea salt and freshly ground black pepper

FOR THE PICKLING LIQUOR
2 tbsp demerara sugar
125ml white wine vinegar
2 cloves

FOR THE ALMOND BUTTER
120g flaked almonds
3–5 tbsp olive oil

1. Cut each cauliflower head in half, top to bottom and through the core. Cut 12 thin slices from both the halved (flat) edges, about 3mm in thickness. Cutting through the stem, cut the rest of the cauliflower into florets. Place the thin slices in a large, shallow heatproof dish.

2. To make the pickled cauliflower, put the sugar, vinegar and cloves in a small saucepan, bring to the boil and boil for 2 minutes. Remove from the heat and pour the pickling liquor over the thin cauliflower slices. Cover with clingfilm and set aside while you roast the remaining cauliflower and make the almond butter.

3. Preheat the oven to 220°C/200°C fan/gas 7.

4. Place the cauliflower florets in a large roasting tray and scatter the cubed butter on top. Season generously with salt and pepper and cover the entire tray with foil. Bake in the oven for 12 minutes, remove the foil and continue to bake for a further 20 minutes, basting the cauliflower with the butter twice during the cooking time, until the cauliflower florets are golden and tender.

5. To make the almond butter, put the flaked almonds in a roasting tray and bake in the oven for 7–8 minutes, until dark golden, shaking the tray halfway through. Remove from the oven, set 20g of the roasted, flaked almonds aside, then put the remaining 100g in a blender with the olive oil and blitz until they reach the consistency of loose nut butter. Season well.

6. When the cauliflower florets are cooked, place them on a large serving platter. Add the chives to the roasting tray and place back in the oven for 1 minute, to gently wilt them, then spoon them over the cauliflower. Drizzle the almond butter over the top and top with the pickled cauliflower slices and reserved toasted almonds.

Crispy Courgettes with Goats' Cheese and Lavender Honey

SERVES: 4 AS A STARTER OR SNACK | PREP TIME: 20 MINUTES, PLUS OVERNIGHT INFUSING | COOKING TIME: 25 MINUTES

Courgettes seem to grow in abundance in my garden, especially in prolonged heat, like we had in summer 2018, when I ended up with quite a few marrows as I didn't pick them soon enough. I enjoy using the plants' flowers too, which I stuff with this goats' cheese mix, coat in batter and fry.

200g soft goats' cheese
1 tbsp finely chopped marjoram or
  oregano
grated zest of ½ lemon
4 courgettes, cut into 5mm-thick rounds
vegetable oil, for deep-frying
sea salt and freshly ground black pepper

FOR THE LAVENDER HONEY
6 tbsp runny honey
2 heads of lavender flowers

FOR THE TEMPURA BATTER
100g cornflour
100g plain flour, plus extra for dusting
generous pinch of salt
130–140ml soda water

1. The day before you want to make and serve the dish, place the honey in a small clean jar. Break up the lavender flowers and add them to the honey. Cover and leave in a warm place to infuse.

2. Put the goats' cheese, marjoram or oregano, lemon zest and a pinch each of salt and pepper in a small food processor and blitz (or put them in a bowl and use a stick blender) until semi smooth.

3. To make the tempura batter, mix the cornflour and flour together in a bowl with the salt. Gradually whisk in enough of the soda water to make a thick batter.

4. Pour enough vegetable oil into a deep saucepan or deep-fat fryer to come up to about 5cm and place over medium heat. If using a deep-fat fryer or if you have a thermometer, heat the oil to 170°C. If not, to check the oil is at the right temperature, drop a 2–3cm cube of bread into the hot oil – it should turn golden and crisp in 1 minute.

5. Season the courgette slices with salt then dust them with flour. One by one, dip them in the tempura batter and, straight away, carefully place them in the hot oil. Fry in batches for 3–4 minutes until golden and crisp. Remove with a slotted spoon, shake off any excess oil and transfer to kitchen paper. Season again with salt while they are hot.

6. Place the fried courgettes on a large serving plate and dollop the goats' cheese on top, then drizzle with the lavender honey. Serve immediately, while they are hot and crispy!

MARCUS' TIP:
If goats' cheese is not to your liking, soft cream cheese works well, or mild Cheddar grated and mixed with a little mascarpone.

Tomato, Wild Garlic and Burrata Salad

SERVES: 4 AS A SUMMER LUNCH OR STARTER | PREP TIME: 15 MINUTES

Wild garlic grows like a weed in the right environment – it likes a little dampness – and the smell of it always signifies that spring is on the way. It does have a relatively short season, however, and once it's gone, it's gone. When it isn't available, use chives instead. They are a great substitute. Any leftover dressing will keep well in the fridge for up to 2 days.

8–12 tomatoes
4 x 100g or 2 x 200g balls of burrata
sea salt and freshly ground black pepper

FOR THE WILD GARLIC DRESSING
2 tbsp pine nuts
16 wild garlic leaves, or 1 bunch of chives
125ml olive oil, plus extra for drizzling
2 tbsp white wine vinegar
1 tsp wholegrain mustard

1. Preheat the oven to 200°C/180°C fan/gas 6.

2. Put the pine nuts on a baking tray and toast them in the oven for 6 minutes, shaking the tray halfway through, then remove from the oven and leave to cool.

3. Put all of the ingredients for the wild garlic dressing in a small blender or food processor and pulse until a chunky dressing is formed. Season to taste with salt and pepper.

4. Cut the tomatoes into slices and wedges, and season well with salt and pepper. Arrange them on serving plates and spoon half of the wild garlic dressing on top.

5. Just before serving, cut the burrata balls in half, if using 100g balls, or into quarters if using 200g balls and place the cut burrata on the plates with the tomatoes. Season the inside of the balls with a little more salt and pepper then spoon over the remaining dressing.

MARCUS' TIP:
Keep tomatoes out of the fridge, until they are becoming overripe, and never serve a cold tomato, as the flavour is dulled.

Chilled Summer Garden Soup
with Lemon and Mackerel

SERVES: 4 | PREP TIME: 40 MINUTES

I created this refreshing soup when I had an abundance of beautiful vegetables in my garden, and the weather was very warm, so turning on the oven was not really on the agenda! This recipe features the vegetables I used, but please regard it just as a guide and feel free to use what you have in abundance, or available in your fridge. I use the whole pea pods in this recipe as they contain lots of juice and flavour. The mackerel – a little bit of luxury on the top – is simply cured, so ensure it is as fresh as possible, or use smoked mackerel instead.

FOR THE SUMMER GARDEN SOUP

16 tender peas in their pods (tops and strings removed) (about 130g)
1 cucumber, skin on, roughly chopped (about 250g)
2 pickled gherkins (40g)
50ml gherkin pickling liquor
100g day-old sliced bread (preferably sourdough), torn
2 courgettes, grated (about 475g)
½ bunch of chives
½ bunch of dill
1 iceberg lettuce, cored and roughly chopped (about 250g)
100g Greek yoghurt
25ml olive oil
8 ice cubes
sea salt and freshly ground black pepper

FOR THE MACKEREL

grated zest and juice of 2 lemons
50ml gherkin pickling liquor
4 mackerel fillets, pin-boned and skin on, cut into 5mm-thick slices

1. Put the peas (including pods), cucumber, gherkins and gherkin pickle liquor in a blender or food processor and blitz until as smooth as possible. Pass through a fine sieve, retaining the liquid. Add the torn bread and leave for 10 minutes.

2. Place the liquid with the bread in the blender or food processor with the remaining ingredients for the soup and blitz until smooth. Season well.

3. For the mackerel, mix the lemon zest and juice into the pickling liquor. Season the mackerel with salt and place in a shallow dish. Pour over the liquid and leave for 10 minutes, then strain off the liquid.

4. Serve the soup in bowls with the mackerel on top.

Asparagus with Bagna Cáuda and Parmesan

SERVES: 4–6 AS A STARTER | PREP TIME: 10 MINUTES | COOKING TIME: 1 HOUR

The arrival of British asparagus is one of the first signs of spring that I most look forward to, and I like to take advantage of its fleeting season as often as possible. Bagna cáuda originates from Piedmont in Italy and is traditionally a pungent sauce made with anchovies, olive oil and garlic. It pairs so well with the delicate flavour and texture of asparagus. Heaped with freshly shaved Parmesan, it is a dish I can eat over and over again.

2–3 bunches of asparagus (500–750g), tough ends trimmed
Parmesan, shaved, to serve

FOR THE BAGNA CÁUDA
6 garlic cloves, peeled
2 shallots, peeled and halved
8 good-quality anchovy fillets in oil
150ml olive oil
50g butter
grated zest and juice of 1 lemon
½ tsp Dijon mustard

1. To make the bagna cáuda, place all ingredients in a small saucepan. Place over low heat, bring to a very low simmer and cook uncovered for 1 hour, until the garlic is soft. Remove from the heat and blend until smooth with a stick blender.

2. Remove the woody ends from the asparagus and blanch in a pan of salted water for 3 minutes, then drain.

3. Place the asparagus in a large serving dish, drizzle liberally with the bagna cáuda and top with Parmesan shavings. Serve immediately.

MARCUS' TIP:
If you are not a fan of anchovies, replace them with 8 large pitted Gordal olives, finely chopped.

Roasted Jerusalem Artichokes
with Prunes, Lentils and Sour Cream

SERVES: 4–6 | PREP TIME: 30 MINUTES | COOKING TIME: ABOUT 1 HOUR

Jerusalem artichokes are one of the vegetables that people seem most averse to cooking with at home. This recipe should turn you into an instant fan of this root vegetable – when roasted until dark and crispy, it has a wonderful sweet nuttiness that is rather addictive. We grow them on the farm and I didn't know what they looked like in the ground – they're massive! The prunes add sweetness, the lentils add earthiness and the sour cream brings welcome acidity to this rich dish.

150g puy or green lentils, rinsed
2.5kg Jerusalem artichokes, well scrubbed
4 tbsp vegetable oil
100g pitted prunes
½ tsp ground cinnamon
200ml milk
150g sour cream
½ bunch of coriander leaves, chopped
½ tsp sumac
sea salt and freshly ground black pepper

1. Preheat the oven to 220°C/200°C fan/gas 7 and cook the lentils according to the packet instructions.

2. Place the scrubbed artichokes and vegetable oil in a large roasting tray, toss to coat the artichokes in the oil, and season with salt and pepper. Roast in the oven for 40–50 minutes, depending on the size of the artichokes, stirring them every 10 minutes, until they are dark golden and crispy on the outside and the centres are soft. Remove from the oven and allow to cool slightly, then cut the artichokes in half and place them back in the roasting tray to keep warm, adding a little more salt and pepper.

3. While the artichokes are roasting, put the prunes and cinnamon in a small saucepan. Cover with enough water to just submerge the prunes, add a little salt, bring to a simmer and cook for 10–15 minutes until the prunes have absorbed the water. Transfer the contents of the pan to a blender or food processor and blitz until smooth. Set aside.

4. Take a quarter of the roasted artichokes and place them in a large saucepan with the milk. Bring to a simmer over medium-high heat and cook for 10 minutes until the artichokes have absorbed the milk. Transfer to a blender or food processor and blitz until smooth, adding a little more salt if needed.

5. To serve, spoon the warm artichoke purée onto a large serving plate. Top with the warm lentils (reheated if necessary), then the remaining roasted artichokes. Dot the prune purée around and spoon over the sour cream. Finish with the chopped coriander, sprinkle over the sumac and serve immediately.

Carrots with Pine Nuts and Tarragon

SERVES: 4 | PREP TIME: 20 MINUTES | COOKING TIME: 25 MINUTES

Carrots are a vegetable we sometimes take for granted, but they are so full of flavour, colour and texture. Forming the base of any good classic gravy, they add a sweetness unlike most other vegetables. To show them off at their best here, I serve them three ways: roasted, pickled and just lightly seasoned, and make a vinaigrette from the carrot juice. It all adds up to create a very delicious dish. The flavour combination with the tarragon is a simple marriage made in heaven.

12 large or 16 medium bunched carrots, washed, tops removed (a few tops reserved)
2 tbsp vegetable oil
1 star anise
120g pine nuts
2 tbsp picked tarragon leaves
sea salt and freshly ground black pepper

FOR THE PICKLING LIQUOR
100ml white wine vinegar
2 tbsp honey

FOR THE VINAIGRETTE
100ml carrot juice (fresh or shop-bought)
3 coriander seeds
1 tbsp rice wine vinegar
50ml olive oil

1. Preheat the oven to 210°C/190°C fan/gas 7.

2. Cut half of the carrots in half, lengthways. Thinly slice the remaining carrots and put half aside to pickle.

3. To make the pickling liquor, place the vinegar and honey in a small saucepan and bring to a simmer. Put half the sliced carrots in a heatproof bowl, pour the hot pickling liquor over the carrots and set aside.

4. Coat the halved carrots with the vegetable oil and season well with salt, pepper and half of the star anise, grated over the carrots using a Microplane or other fine grater. Place in a roasting tray and roast in the oven for 20–25 minutes until golden, tossing them once halfway through the cooking time.

5. Place the pine nuts on a baking tray and toast in the oven for 8–10 minutes until a deep golden colour, shaking them halfway through. Remove from the oven and set aside 20g for sprinkling over the finished dish and place the rest in a small blender. Season with salt, add 2–4 tablespoons of water and blitz to form a purée – it should have a slightly looser texture than peanut butter. Set aside.

6. To make the vinaigrette, put the carrot juice in a medium saucepan with the coriander seeds and remaining half of the star anise and bring to the boil. Simmer rapidly for a few minutes, until the liquid has reduced to around 25ml, then remove from the heat and strain into a small bowl. Mix in the rice wine vinegar and olive oil, and season with salt.

7. To assemble the dish, place the remaining sliced carrots in a bowl and dress them with the carrot vinaigrette. Spoon the pine nut purée onto 4 plates. Top with the warm roasted carrots, pickled carrots and dressed carrots. Finish with the remaining toasted pine nuts, some reserved carrot tops and the tarragon leaves.

Parsnip, Rosemary and Horseradish Gratin

SERVES: 4 | PREP TIME: 15 MINUTES
COOKING TIME: 1¼ HOURS, PLUS 30 MINUTES INFUSING

This can be a side or a main dish. Gratins are one of the best comfort foods around, and a handy thing to cook given all the preparation can be done in advance of when you need to serve it. You can even bake it a couple of days ahead, then reheat to serve. I like to serve this with roast chicken or braised meat on a cold winter's night.

225ml single cream
525ml milk
½ onion, thinly sliced
½ nutmeg, finely grated
2 bay leaves
½ bunch of rosemary, leaves stripped
1 tsp table salt
4 tbsp fresh grated horseradish or 4 tbsp
   horseradish sauce
6 large parsnips, peeled and cut into
   5mm-thick slices

1. Put the cream, milk, onion, nutmeg, bay leaves, rosemary leaves and salt in a medium saucepan. Bring to a simmer and cook gently for 15 minutes then remove from the heat and blend using a stick blender until the herbs have broken down. Cover the surface of the mixture with clingfilm and leave to infuse for 30 minutes, then pass it through a fine sieve and retain the liquid. Stir through the grated horseradish or horseradish sauce.

2. Preheat the oven to 200°C/180°C fan/gas 6.

3. Place a layer of parsnip slices on the bottom of a 20 × 20cm baking dish, then cover with a little of the milk mixture. Repeat, ensuring the parsnips are fully submerged in the liquid. Cover the entire dish with foil and bake for 25 minutes. Remove the foil and bake for a further 20–25 minutes until a knife inserted into the gratin meets no resistance.

4. Remove from the oven and serve.

MARCUS' TIP:
I prefer a roast dinner with one side done really well, rather than three or four different vegetables on the plate – one great dish like this one that has a bit more effort put into it makes it much more interesting. Nothing wrong with that.

Celeriac, Ham Hock and Barley Hot Pot

SERVES: 4–6 | PREP TIME: 10 MINUTES
COOKING TIME: ABOUT 3¾ HOURS

As far as winter warmers go, this one ticks all the boxes. Celeriac is such a versatile ingredient, to serve both raw and cooked. It is a winter staple for me and it pairs well with the salty, rich ham hock in this recipe. Just add some fresh bread and you have a great winter's lunch or supper. Always remember to bring ham hocks to the boil in a pan of water then drain them before cooking, otherwise they will be too salty.

1 smoked ham hock (about 1kg)
½ bunch of thyme, tied with string
200g pearl barley, rinsed
100g yellow split peas, rinsed
1 celeriac, peeled and roughly chopped
4 onions, roughly chopped
4 carrots, peeled and roughly chopped
1 leek, rinsed and roughly chopped
½ bunch of flat-leaf parsley, leaves
　roughly chopped
freshly ground black pepper

1. Place the ham hock in a large saucepan and cover with cold water. Bring to the boil, then drain and rinse the ham under cold running water. Place the ham back in the pan, cover with fresh cold water and add the thyme and a generous grind of black pepper. Place over medium heat, bring to a simmer and cook, uncovered, for 2½ hours, topping up the water to ensure the ham is always submerged.

2. Add the pearl barley and split peas and cook for a further 30 minutes.

3. Check to see if the hock is cooked by putting the handle of a spoon into the flesh: if the handle meets no resistance, the meat is cooked. If the meat doesn't yet yield to the spoon handle, continue to cook it, checking every 15 minutes. Remove the hock, add the remaining ingredients, apart from the parsley, and simmer for a further 30 minutes.

4. Using two forks, remove the skin from the hock, discard it and shred the meat. Return the meat to the pot and simmer gently for 5 minutes. Check the seasoning and adjust if necessary. Remove the bunch of thyme.

5. Finish with the parsley and serve.

Poached Rhubarb and Rhubarb Jelly with Bay Leaf Cream and Shortbread

SERVES: 6 | PREP TIME: 25 MINUTES, PLUS SETTING AND INFUSING
COOKING TIME: ABOUT 15 MINUTES

Rhubarb, jelly and cream. So simple, yet so delicious. The bay leaf infusion in the cream adds a savoury element to the dish which balances the sweetness of the rhubarb and shortbread. During rhubarb season I generally always have some poached in the fridge – it is great to have with cereal for breakfast, to use in baking and also as a simple pudding. Who doesn't like rhubarb and jelly?

200g caster sugar
2 tbsp grenadine
400g rhubarb stalks, trimmed and cut into 4cm lengths
3 gelatine leaves

FOR THE BAY LEAF CREAM
100ml milk
2 bay leaves
300ml double cream

FOR THE SHORTBREAD
70g plain flour
50g cornflour
40g icing sugar, sifted
pinch of sea salt
90g cold diced butter

MARCUS' TIP:
Make a double batch of shortbread and freeze half of the dough, ready to bake another day.

1. To cook the rhubarb, put the caster sugar and grenadine in a large saucepan. Top up with 500ml water and bring to a simmer over medium heat, stirring to dissolve the sugar. Place the rhubarb pieces in the hot liquid and simmer for 5 minutes, then remove the pan from the heat and allow the rhubarb to continue to cook in the liquid for 10 minutes, as it cools down. Carefully transfer the rhubarb from the liquid into a bowl using a slotted spoon and place in the fridge to cool. Measure out 400ml of the cooking liquor, place it in a medium saucepan and set aside.

2. To make the jelly, soak the 3 gelatine leaves in a bowl of cold water for 5 minutes. Heat the 400ml of rhubarb cooking liquor until it just reaches the boil, then remove the pan from the heat. Squeeze the excess water from the gelatine leaves and stir them into the hot liquid until completely dissolved. Strain the liquid into a clean container lined with baking parchment (around 15cm square), which gives the jelly at least 1cm height, and chill until set. Remove from the container and cut into squares.

3. For the bay leaf cream, heat the milk in a small saucepan. Break up the bay leaves and add them to the milk. Remove from the heat as soon as it reaches the boil. Cover the surface of the milk with clingfilm and set aside to infuse for 20 minutes. Using a stick blender, blitz the milk to disperse the leaves, strain and place in the fridge to cool. Once cool, mix in the double cream.

4. To make the shortbread, preheat the oven to 200°C/180°C fan/gas 6 and line a baking tray with baking parchment.

5. Put all of the dry ingredients in a food processor and blitz to combine. Add the butter and pulse in short bursts until you have a dough that clumps together in little bits. It may take

some time to incorporate the butter into the dry ingredients. Tip onto a clean surface and work together. Place on the lined baking tray and shape into a rectangle about 6mm thick. Bake in the oven for 10–12 minutes until a pale golden colour. Remove from the oven, allow to cool slightly, then break up into pieces.

6. To serve, divide the the cream and rhubarb pieces among 6 bowls. Top with the jelly and shortbread pieces.

Strawberry and Mint Eton Mess

SERVES 4 | PREP TIME: 25 MINUTES | COOKING TIME: 1 HOUR

Eton mess, said to have originated from Eton when a tray of meringues was dropped on the floor, is a great summer pudding. This is more of a 'make your own mess' pudding – the presentation is neat and tidy then you create your own mess by smashing it. All the fun's inside but you can't initially see it. The mint gives the dish a freshness which helps cut through the sweetness of the meringue.

350g strawberries, hulled
25ml vodka
2 tbsp strawberry jam
200g double cream, lightly whipped
12 mint leaves, finely sliced

FOR THE MERINGUE
1 lemon wedge
4 egg whites, at room temperature
110g caster sugar
110g icing sugar, sifted

1. Preheat the oven to 120°C/100°C fan/gas ½ and line a large baking sheet with non-stick baking parchment. Draw 4 x 10cm circles on the paper.

2. To make the meringue, rub the lemon wedge around the inside of a clean mixing bowl or the bowl of a stand mixer. Add the egg whites and whisk on high speed until they form stiff peaks. Decrease the mixing speed to medium and gradually add the sugar, whisking continuously. Increase to high speed and whisk for 5–10 minutes until you have a stiff meringue and all grains of sugar have dissolved. Add the icing sugar and whisk until well combined.

3. Place the meringue into a piping bag, and pipe into the centre of each circle on the parchment-lined baking sheet to form a dome. Create 3 more domes.

4. Bake in the oven for 40–50 minutes until crisp on the outside, but still soft in the centre. Turn off the oven and leave the door ajar until the meringues are cool to touch. Very gently, scoop out the soft meringue with a spoon, leaving the shell intact. Set the soft meringue aside.

5. Take 200g of the strawberries and blend together with the vodka. Pass through a fine sieve. Chop the remaining 150g of strawberries and add to the soft meringue. Fold in the strawberry jam, whipped cream and finely sliced mint.

6. Divide the strawberry sauce between 4 bowls then carefully fill the meringue shells with the cream mix. Gently place a meringue in each bowl, on top of the sauce. Allow your guests to then make their own mess by smashing the meringue shell with their spoons!

Gooseberry and Basil Fool

SERVES: 4 | PREP TIME: 15 MINUTES | COOKING TIME: 30 MINUTES, PLUS SETTING

When my dad was a young boy, gooseberries were one of his favourite fruits. Gooseberries tend to grow like weeds, and are a great fruit to just pick and pop in the freezer, whole, to save for a rainy and not so warm day. You can use frozen or tinned berries in this recipe, or try them in a crumble. The addition of basil in this recipe brings a slightly savoury note to the fool and creates an even richer floral aroma. You can make these fools up to a day ahead, if you wish.

150g caster sugar
400g gooseberries, topped and tailed
200ml double cream

FOR THE CUSTARD
160ml milk
16 large basil leaves
2 egg yolks
1 tsp custard powder
30g demerara sugar

1. Put the caster sugar in a large saucepan. Add 200ml of warm water and bring to a simmer. Add the gooseberries and simmer gently for 5 minutes, then remove a fifth of the berries and set them aside. Keep cooking the remaining berries for about another 10 minutes until soft. Transfer to a blender or food processor and blitz until smooth.

2. To make the custard, put the milk and half of the basil leaves in a small saucepan and bring just to the boil, stirring frequently.

3. Put the egg yolks, custard powder and sugar in a heatproof bowl and whisk until well combined. Slowly pour in the hot milk mixture, whisking continuously. Return the mixture to the pan and cook over very low heat, stirring constantly, for about 5 minutes or until the custard coats the back of a wooden spoon (take care not to boil the custard as the egg yolks will scramble). Strain through a fine sieve into a clean container, cover the surface of the custard with clingfilm (to avoid a skin forming) and chill in the fridge.

4. Lightly whip the double cream.

5. Once the custard is cold, whisk it well then fold it into the lightly whipped cream. Fold in the gooseberry purée. Thinly slice the remaining basil leaves and fold them through the mix.

6. Divide the fool among 4 glasses. Halve the gooseberries you cooked and set aside, and arrange them on top of the fools. Place in the fridge for at least 1 hour, until set.

Caramelised Honey-roasted Pears
with Mascarpone and Filo

SERVES: 4 | PREP TIME: 20 MINUTES | COOKING TIME: ABOUT 30 MINUTES

One of the wonderful discoveries of Melfort Farm was the honey I inherited. The floral taste is quite remarkable and I found myself wanting to use it in a lot of my cooking. This discovery coincided with the pears ripening too, so it was a no-brainer to combine the two.

8 tbsp runny honey
4 ripe (but not too soft) pears, peeled, quartered and cored
6 sprigs of thyme
20g butter, melted
pinch of sea salt
7 sheets of filo pastry
200g mascarpone
100ml double cream
25ml brandy

1. Preheat the oven to 210°C/190°C fan/gas 7.

2. Place the honey in a roasting tray just large enough to fit the pear quarters in a single layer (about 20 × 20cm). Put the dish in the oven for 5 minutes to warm the honey, then add the pear quarters and thyme and return to the oven for 15–20 minutes, until the pears are golden and cooked through. Remove from the oven, carefully lift out the pears and set them aside. Scrape the honey into a bowl, removing the thyme sprigs and set it aside, too.

3. Add 2 tablespoons of the baked honey to the melted butter in a bowl, along with the salt, and mix well.

4. Take one sheet of filo pastry and brush it with the honey butter. Repeat with the remaining sheets and lay them on top of each other. Cut the large rectangle into 8 equal squares and gently scrunch up the edges of each layered piece. Place them on a baking tray and bake for 8–10 minutes until golden and crisp.

5. In a large bowl, whisk the mascarpone until smooth. Add the double cream, brandy and 2 tablespoons of the baked honey and whisk together until stiff.

6. To serve, place 2 pastry pieces on each plate then add the baked pear quarters. Dollop with the mascarpone and drizzle over the remaining baked honey.

MARCUS' TIP:
Filo pastry is a great ingredient to have on hand in the freezer. You can use it for a speedy pie in winter, or for a summer quiche.

Harvest Preservation

When you have an abundance of fruit or vegetables from the garden it is sometimes hard to know what to do with it all if it is too much to get through in your daily meals. Preserving is something we chefs do quite a lot. It's wonderful coming across a little jar of wonder a month or two down the line when the fresh ingredient is no longer available. And preserved foods tend to just get better and better the longer you keep them. They look great on the kitchen shelves, too – just like a good cookbook. The methods of preservation below detail ways to ensure you can maximise the use, and enjoyment, of seasonal produce. It also means a lot less waste, and plenty to look forward to throughout the year.

For any form of preservation, you will need clean, sterilised glass jars, with clean lids. I find the best way to do this is place the clean jars in an oven, at 140°C/120°C fan/gas 1 for 10 minutes. Clean any non-ovenproof lids and rubber seals separately in hot soapy water, then rinse and dry. Remove the jars from the oven and allow to cool slightly before filling and sealing.

The recipes that follow are meant as guidelines so you can adapt them according to what you have a lot of, or flavours you enjoy. Garden herbs, spices and citrus peel are all great things to add to any of the recipes below.

FERMENTING

Fermentation is an age-old preservation method that has had somewhat of a resurgence of late. It's a little more adventurous, and is something everyone should try. It's good for your gut, too. A lot of items we consume daily are actually a product of fermentation, such as cheese and wine. Kimchi is Korean in origin and is a spicy, fermented cabbage. It is great to shred up and use in salads, on burgers, in frittatas and in toasted sandwiches.

Best for fermenting

Cabbage, Cauliflower leaves, Fennel, Lettuce, Kale

Fennel Kimchi

MAKES: AROUND 1KG | PREPARATION TIME: 20 MINUTES, PLUS 2 WEEKS' FERMENTATION

2 garlic cloves, grated

15cm piece of fresh ginger, peeled and grated

1 tsp demerara sugar

2 tbsp gochujang paste

3 tbsp rice wine vinegar

1 tbsp table salt

3 fennel bulbs (about 900g), cut into 5mm-thick slices

1. Put all of the ingredients, apart from the fennel, in a blender or food processor. Blitz until well combined and a paste has formed.

2. Using gloves, massage the paste into the fennel for at least 4 minutes.

3. Pack the fennel kimchi into sterilised jars and seal with a lid. Leave to ferment at room temperature for at least 2 weeks before eating. The longer you leave it the more developed the flavour will become. To stop the fermentation, place in the fridge.

PICKLING

Jars of pickled produce not only look beautiful, they are also a very tasty thing to have on hand all year round. Always ensure what you are pickling has been thoroughly washed and that all the pieces are of an equal size. I recommend a minimum pickling time of 14 days, but up to 1 year will yield flavoursome results. Make sure you evenly distribute the bay leaves and peppercorns, and any other flavourings you use, between the jars. And always ensure the lids are properly sealed, to prevent any spoilage, along with storing the jars in a cool, dark place.

Best for pickling

Cucumber, Beetroot, Cauliflower, Beans, Cabbage, Rhubarb, Carrots

---

Pickled Cucumbers

MAKES: AROUND 700G | PREPARATION TIME: 10 MINUTES, PLUS CURING AND PICKLING | COOKING TIME: UNDER 5 MINUTES

2 small cucumbers (about 200g each), washed
4 tbsp rock salt

FOR THE PICKLING LIQUOR
250ml white wine vinegar
55g demerara sugar
½ tsp caraway seeds
6 black peppercorns
6 dill sprigs

1. Cut the cucumbers in half widthways, then each half lengthways into four. Put them in a dish, sprinkle them with the rock salt and leave for 2 hours. Wash off the salt and pack into a sterilised jar.

2. Put all ingredients for pickling liquor, apart from the dill, in a medium saucepan and bring to the boil. Simmer for 2 minutes, to dissolve the sugar, then remove from the heat and add the dill.

3. Pour the hot pickling liquor over the cucumbers and seal with a lid. Leave for at least 2 weeks before eating. They will keep for a good few weeks in the fridge once opened.

JAM-MAKING

I have sisters-in-law, brothers-in-law, friends and uncles who all make jam, and everyone makes it completely differently. I wanted to put jams in this book as there is a right way and a wrong way to go about jam-making, and it's all about balance. A big pot of steaming fruit sends delicious aromas throughout the house and is the perfect way to use up overripe fruit. One of the issues we find we have to tackle as parents is the amount of added sugar in shop-bought products. Making your own preserves allows you to control the levels of sugar you add, and thus the end result on your larder shelf. Obviously, fruit that is sourer will need more sugar, but if you combine a few different ones you can get the best of both worlds.

Best for jam

Stone fruit, Berries, Rhubarb, Figs, Quince

Fig Jam

MAKES: 1.3KG | PREPARATION TIME: 15 MINUTES | COOKING TIME: ABOUT 30 MINUTES

1kg figs, tops of stalks removed, roughly chopped
2 fig leaves, cleaned
500g jam sugar (containing pectin)

1. Put all the ingredients in a large saucepan and stir well to combine. Place over low heat and allow the sugar to dissolve, then increase the heat slightly and bring to a gentle simmer.

2. Once the liquid begins to come out of the figs, turn the heat up a little and stir regularly to prevent the jam catching on the bottom of the pan. Simmer rapidly until the jam reaches 105°. If you don't have a thermometer, use the saucer test: put a saucer in the freezer, then once it's cold put half a teaspoon of the jam on the saucer. If it does not run, it's ready.

3. Remove the fig leaves, scraping the jam off them and back into the pan, and pour the jam into sterilised jars. Cover with the lids immediately. The unopened jars will keep for up to 12 months, and up to 1 month in the fridge once opened.

CHUTNEY MAKING

We always have chutney in my house, whether it's homemade or shop-bought. It is a staple on cheese sandwiches and a go-to condiment when a little extra flavour is needed.

Best for chutney

Tomatoes, Onions, Stone fruit, Apples, Pears, Rhubarb, Figs

Apple, Rhubarb and Rosemary Chutney

MAKES: 475G | PREPARATION TIME: 15 MINUTES
COOKING TIME: 40 MINUTES

1 onion, cut into 1cm dice
2 apples, peeled, cored and cut into 2cm dice (about 400g)
4 rhubarb stalks, cut into 2cm pieces (about 250g)
4 sprigs of rosemary, tied together with string
150ml white wine vinegar
100g dried, pitted dates, finely chopped

1. Put all the ingredients in a medium saucepan over medium heat. Bring to a simmer and cook gently for 30–40 minutes until sticky and shiny.

2. Remove the rosemary sprigs, pour into sterilised jars and seal. The unopened jars will keep for up to 12 months, and up to 1 month in the fridge once opened.

Beetroot, Wasabi, Feta and Pine Nut Salad

Field Mushroom, Walnut and Thyme Filo Pie

Roasted Cauliflower and Walnut Tagliatelle

Chargrilled Mackerel, Pickled Onions and Salsa Verde

Green Chilli Salsa Cod with Roast Potato and Almond Salad

Baked Haddock with Lentils, Basil and Mascarpone

Thai Chicken Salad

Chicken, Leek and Wholegrain Mustard Potato Pie

Chicken, Split Pea and Kale Curry

Hasselback Potatoes with Red Wine and Pork Ragu

Rump Steak with Green Sauce and Beer-braised Onions

Pancetta and Mushroom Pasta Bake

Pork Chops with Green Olives, Baked Orange and Fennel

Beef, Asparagus, Cashew and Miso Stir-fry

Lamb Chops with Minted Orzo and Pea Salad

Lamb Meatballs with Harissa and Sour Cream

Weekday Suppers

Weekday Suppers

Weekday meals are some of the toughest to get inspired for. They're the ones we don't think about until we get home or call for a takeout. Or we eat something quick and rubbish because we just don't have time to prep a meal. We're all working incredibly hard, and we also have to fit in travel, family and down time, so making food can quickly become a chore. These simplified dishes are really easy to make, and they offer great nutritional value, too. Don't overthink it and don't worry about it.

Beetroot, Wasabi, Feta and Pine Nut Salad

SERVES 4 | PREP TIME: 25 MINUTES | COOKING TIME: 1 HOUR

This dish makes a great summer, or early autumn, meal. It is delicious and also surprisingly filling, with the chickpeas, feta and pine nuts all playing a part. The wasabi is there to season the dish, not to overpower it. So even if you are not a fan, do try it!

100g pine nuts
500g cooked beetroot
100g tinned chickpeas, drained, rinsed
    and roughly chopped
100g lamb's lettuce
200g feta
2 slices of sourdough (about 100g), gently
    toasted then torn
sea salt and freshly ground black pepper

FOR THE DRESSING
½ tsp wasabi paste
50ml olive oil
1 tbsp rice wine vinegar

1. Preheat the oven to 210°C/190°C fan/gas 7.

2. Place the pine nuts on a baking tray and toast in the oven for 8–10 minutes, shaking halfway through, until a deep golden colour.

3. Slice the beetroot into large chunks and lay them on a platter. Scatter the chopped chickpeas on top, followed by the lamb's lettuce. Crumble the feta on top, then add the pine nuts and a generous grind of black pepper. Finish with the torn sourdough pieces.

4. For the dressing, whisk everything together in a bowl, season with salt, then drizzle over the top of the salad. Serve immediately.

Field Mushroom, Walnut and Thyme Filo Pie

SERVES: 4–6 | PREP TIME: 25 MINUTES | COOKING TIME: 55 MINUTES

I'm from the North and two things I really love are pies and mushrooms. This is rich, satisfying and a total winner, providing a delicious weekday supper or weekend lunch. It's technically a little challenging, but once you've got the hang of it, it's simple to put together. In summer, a side of chargrilled broccoli makes a great accompaniment, and in winter I like it with kale sautéed in a little butter and soy sauce.

100g puy lentils
70g butter
2 onions, thinly sliced
1 garlic clove, finely grated
½ bunch of thyme, ⅔ of it tied together with string, the remaining third's leaves picked
8 large field (or flat) mushrooms, thinly sliced
100g walnuts
1 tbsp vegetable oil
100g cream cheese
2 tbsp milk
50g Cheddar cheese, grated
7 large sheets of filo pastry
sea salt and freshly ground black pepper

1. Cook the lentils according to the packet instructions.

2. Melt 15g of the butter in a large frying pan over medium heat, add the onions, garlic, tied thyme and season well with salt and pepper. Cook for about 15 minutes until lightly browned, then transfer to a large bowl. Heat another 15g of the butter in the same frying pan, with the bunch of tied thyme, and when the butter has melted, add the mushrooms and season well with salt. Cook for about 15 minutes, until all of the liquid has evaporated. Transfer the cooked mushrooms to the bowl containing the onions. Squeeze any liquid out of the bunch of thyme into the bowl then discard.

3. Preheat the oven to 220°C/200°C fan/gas 7.

4. Put the walnut pieces in a roasting dish with the vegetable oil. Season well with salt, toss to coat in the oil and toast in the oven for 5–7 minutes until a deep golden colour. Remove from the oven, leave to cool then roughly chop.

5. Add the walnuts, lentils and thyme leaves to the large bowl. Mix well. In a separate bowl, whisk the cream cheese and milk together until smooth. Add to the large bowl, along with the grated Cheddar, and mix well.

6. Melt the remaining 40g of butter in a pan. Brush a 23cm pie dish with a little butter. Lay one sheet of pastry on your work surface, brush liberally with melted butter and place in the dish. Brush a second piece of filo with butter then add in an overlapping criss-cross pattern. Continue with 2 more buttered sheets to create a star shape. Add the mushroom mixture and smooth the surface. Brush the remaining 3 filo sheets with butter, then scrunch up and place on top of the pie. Bake in the oven for 20–25 minutes, until the pastry is golden and the mushroom mix is lightly bubbling.

7. Remove from the oven and serve warm with your chosen side dish.

Roasted Cauliflower and Walnut Tagliatelle

SERVES: 4 | PREP TIME: 15 MINUTES | COOKING TIME: ABOUT 50 MINUTES

Well-roasted cauliflower has the most delicious, nutty flavour. I always find that home cooks do not roast it for long enough, thus missing out on the best flavour from it. This recipe combines a roasted cauliflower purée to create the sauce, with roasted florets and crunchy, toasted walnuts.

1 large cauliflower, leaves removed,
  broken into florets
50g butter, cubed
100g walnut pieces
1 tbsp vegetable oil
150ml milk
150ml good-quality vegetable stock
350g tagliatelle
200g cavolo nero, roughly chopped
¼ bunch of flat-leaf parsley, leaves
  chopped
sea salt and freshly ground black pepper

1. Preheat the oven to 230°C/210°C fan/gas 8.

2. Place the cauliflower florets in a roasting dish with the cubed butter. Season well with salt and pepper and bake in the oven for 6 minutes. Stir well, to coat the cauliflower in the butter, and cook for a further 20 minutes, stirring again after 10 minutes. The cauliflower should be a dark golden brown by this point. If it's not, return it to the oven for a further 5 minutes.

3. While the cauliflower is roasting, put the walnut pieces in another roasting dish with the vegetable oil. Season well with salt, toss to coat in the oil and toast in the oven for 5–7 minutes until a deep golden colour. Remove from the oven, leave to cool then roughly chop.

4. Pour the milk and stock into a medium saucepan and bring to the boil. Add a third of the toasted walnuts and simmer for 5 minutes, then add a third of the roasted cauliflower florets and simmer for a further 5 minutes. Remove from the heat, transfer to a blender or food processor and blitz until silky smooth. Taste, and add more salt if necessary.

5. Bring a medium-large saucepan of salted water to the boil. Cook the tagliatelle according to the packet instructions, adding the cavolo nero for the last minute of cooking. Drain, reserving a little of the pasta water.

6. Mix the tagliatelle and cavolo nero with the roasted cauliflower and walnut sauce. Add a little pasta water to your sauce to loosen it a little if desired. Stir through the remaining roasted cauliflower and toasted nuts and parsley and serve.

Chargrilled Mackerel, Pickled Onions and Salsa Verde

SERVES: 4 | PREP TIME: ABOUT 15 MINUTES, PLUS SOAKING AND PICKLING

COOKING TIME: 5–10 MINUTES

There is not much that beats freshly caught mackerel that has been lightly chargrilled on the barbecue or on a griddle pan. The quick pickled onions are a great, speedy, addition to the dish, giving it extra texture and acidity, and will keep happily in the fridge for up to 2 weeks. I like to serve the mackerel with some steamed new potatoes and a peppery rocket salad.

1 tbsp vegetable oil
8 mackerel fillets, pin-boned, skin scored
sea salt and freshly ground black pepper

FOR THE QUICK PICKLED ONIONS

2 small red onions, sliced into 3mm-thick rings
100ml pickled gherkin liquid
2 tbsp caper brine
100ml white wine vinegar
4 tbsp honey
1 tbsp onion seeds

FOR THE SALSA VERDE

2 heaped tbsp finely chopped tarragon leaves
¼ bunch of flat-leaf parsley, leaves picked
20g drained capers in brine
grated zest and juice of 1 lemon
125ml extra virgin olive oil

1. To make the pickled onions, separate the onion rings from each other and place them in a bowl of cold water. Leave to soak for 10 minutes, then drain and transfer to a shallow heatproof dish. Place all other ingredients for the pickled onions in a small saucepan and bring to the boil. Pour the hot pickle mix over the onions and cover the dish with clingfilm. Set aside.

2. To make the salsa verde, put all the ingredients in a mini food processor or blender and pulse until you have a chunky sauce. Add salt to taste and set aside.

3. If using a barbecue, preheat it until hot. If using a griddle pan, place it over high heat until almost smoking. Brush the vegetable oil onto the mackerel fillets, on both sides. Season the skin side with salt and pepper and place on the hot barbecue or griddle, skin-side down, for 2 minutes (in batches if you're using a griddle pan). Season the flesh side then carefully turn the fillets over and cook for a further 2–3 minutes.

4. Serve immediately, with a good dollop of the salsa verde and the pickled onions.

MARCUS' TIP:
Salsa verde literally translates as 'green sauce'. This is the traditional Italian version, but you can use the same quantities of different herbs, such as coriander, mint or lemon balm, to create delicious sauces depending upon what's in your fridge or herb pots.

Green Chilli Salsa Cod with Roast Potato and Almond Salad

SERVES: 4 | PREP TIME: 15 MINUTES | COOKING TIME: 35 MINUTES

Weekday suppers are all about meals that are delicious, but time friendly. In some ways, these ingredients shouldn't go together – cod is classically English, roast potatoes too, but then the salsa and the almond salad hail from somewhere quite different – but it's my job to be daring. Cod is a meaty fish and can carry all of those elements brilliantly, working a treat with the salsa, which brings a lovely, spicy freshness to this rich dish, balancing it well.

2 tbsp olive oil
4 skinless cod fillets (about 150g each)
sea salt and freshly ground black pepper

FOR THE GREEN CHILLI SALSA

grated zest and juice of 1 lime
1 garlic clove, finely grated
1 small green chilli, deseeded and roughly
   chopped
2 tbsp rice wine vinegar
2 tbsp chopped coriander leaves, plus 2
   tbsp for the potato salad
2 tbsp chopped mint leaves
60ml olive oil

FOR THE ROAST POTATO AND ALMOND SALAD

500g small potatoes, scrubbed
4 tbsp olive oil
100g almonds
75g good-quality mayonnaise

1. Preheat the oven to 210°C/190°C fan/gas 7.

2. First, cook the potatoes. Toss them in the olive oil and season with salt and pepper. Place in a large roasting tray and bake in the oven for 25 minutes. Add the almonds and bake for a further 8–10 minutes, until the potatoes are cooked and the almonds are toasted.

3. To make the salsa, blend all the ingredients together in a small food processor, or in a jug or bowl with a stick blender, until smooth. Season to taste with salt and pepper.

4. Heat the 2 tablespoons of olive oil for the fish in a large non-stick frying pan over medium heat. Season the cod fillets with salt and pepper on each side then place them in the hot oil. Cook for 3–4 minutes until golden brown, then gently flip them over and cook for a further 3–4 minutes to brown the other side, until the fish is cooked through. Remove the pan from the heat and add the green chilli salsa to the pan, spooning it over the fish. Leave to rest for 2 minutes.

5. To serve, mix the 2 tablespoons of coriander for the salad into the mayonnaise along with 2 tablespoons of cold water to thin it down to drizzling consistency. Roughly chop the almonds. Combine the warm roasted potatoes with the chopped, roasted almonds, place on a large serving dish and drizzle with the mayonnaise. Finish with a generous twist of black pepper.

6. Serve the salad immediately, alongside the fish.

Baked Haddock with Lentils, Basil and Mascarpone

SERVES: 4 | PREP TIME: 10 MINUTES | COOKING TIME: 50 MINUTES

This dish is a comforting one-pot wonder, as well as being extremely easy to make. Just serve it with some green vegetables on the side, such as broccoli or kale, and you have a complete meal ready to go. You can use cod or hake instead of haddock, too – whichever is available to you (it's useful to keep fish fillets in the freezer for dishes like this). You can also use pre-cooked lentils.

4 skinless, boneless haddock fillets
   (about 150g each)
4 tbsp rock salt
2 tbsp vegetable oil
2 onions, thinly sliced
1 garlic clove, crushed
1 tsp sweet smoked paprika
2 tbsp tomato purée
250ml tomato juice
600ml good-quality chicken or
   vegetable stock
250g puy lentils, well rinsed
1 tbsp olive oil
100g mascarpone
2 tbsp milk
grated zest of ½ lemon
½ bunch of basil, leaves picked
sea salt and freshly ground black pepper

1. Cover the haddock fillets with the rock salt and refrigerate for 10 minutes, then rinse the salt off under cold running water and pat the fish dry with kitchen paper. Set aside.

2. Preheat the oven to 200°C/180°C fan/gas 6.

3. Heat the vegetable oil in a large casserole dish over medium heat. Add the sliced onions, season well with salt and pepper and cook for about 10 minutes, until soft, then add the garlic and cook for a further 3 minutes. Stir in the smoked paprika, followed by the tomato purée. Cook for 1 minute, then mix in the tomato juice and stock. Season again with salt and pepper and bring to the boil. Add the lentils, mix well, cover the casserole dish with a lid, or foil, and place in the oven for 20 minutes, stirring after 10 minutes.

4. Remove the casserole from the oven. Remove the lid or foil and place the salted haddock fillets into the lentils, pressing them down with a spoon so they are almost submerged. Drizzle the olive oil on top of the fillets. Pop the lid, or foil, back on top and return the casserole to the oven for 10 minutes. Remove from the oven and leave to rest for a further 5 minutes, covered, until the fish has cooked through.

5. Place the mascarpone in a bowl with the milk, lemon zest and a pinch each of salt and pepper and whisk until smooth. Dollop on top of the fish and lentils. Pop the casserole back in the oven for 2 minutes then serve, sprinkled with the basil leaves.

MARCUS' TIP:
Salting white fish with rock salt seasons the fish right the way through, while also removing some of the water content. Leave the salt on the fish for maximum 10 minutes, before rinsing it off (5 minutes for thinner fish).

Thai Chicken Salad

SERVES: 4 | PREP TIME: 20 MINUTES, PLUS MARINATING
COOKING TIME: 15 MINUTES, PLUS RESTING

I am sure everyone has their own version of their favourite Thai chicken salad. This is mine. I really enjoy the freshness of the lime and coriander, and the savoury richness that the toasted peanuts add. My kids love the noodles, but not too much heat, so I tend to scatter extra chilli on top of mine after serving. To maximise the flavour, I suggest marinating the chicken breasts the night before, though you can skip this step (or marinate for a shorter time) if you're in a hurry.

3 boneless, skinless chicken breasts
100g unsalted peanuts, roughly chopped
200g rice noodles
2 medium carrots, peeled and cut into
    thin strips
1 cucumber, cut into thin strips
200g beansprouts
½ bunch of coriander, leaves picked
¼ bunch of mint, leaves picked
red chillies, sliced, to serve (optional)

FOR THE MARINADE
4 tbsp coconut cream
1 tsp red curry paste
1 tsp white miso paste

FOR THE DRESSING
100ml rice wine vinegar
25g palm sugar, grated, or soft brown
    sugar
50ml fish sauce
100ml toasted sesame oil
2 tbsp tamarind paste
2 lemongrass stalks, tough outer layers
    removed, inner layers grated with a fine
    or Microplane grater
4cm piece of fresh ginger, peeled and
    grated with a fine or Microplane grater
2 tbsp peanut butter
grated zest and juice of 1 lime

1. Whisk together the marinade ingredients in a small bowl. Put the chicken breasts in a dish, coat them in the marinade and refrigerate for at least an hour (ideally overnight).

2. Preheat the oven to 220°C/200°C fan/gas 7.

3. Lay a sheet of foil on your work surface. Place the marinated chicken on top then gather the foil around it. Place the foil package on a baking tray and bake in the oven for 15 minutes. Put the peanuts on a separate baking tray and roast in the oven for 5–7 minutes. Remove the nuts and chicken and allow the chicken to cool in the foil for 20 minutes, then unwrap and slice.

4. Place the rice noodles in a large heatproof bowl and bring a kettleful of water to the boil. Cover the noodles in the boiling water and leave to sit for 10 minutes.

5. Blitz all the dressing ingredients together in a blender, or in a jug using a stick blender.

6. Drain the noodles and place them in a large bowl. Add the carrots, cucumber and beansprouts and mix well. Arrange on a large serving platter then top with the chicken and the dressing. Finish with the coriander, mint and peanuts (and sliced chillies, to taste, if using).

MARCUS' TIP:
Make a double batch of the dressing and keep it in a jar in the fridge for up to 2 days. It is great to have on hand for coleslaw or a quick vegetable stir-fry.

Chicken, Leek and Wholegrain Mustard Potato Pie

SERVES: 4–6 | PREP TIME: 25 MINUTES, PLUS COOLING
COOKING TIME: 50 MINUTES

This is a great dish when you need something substantial and warming for supper during the week. Use leftover cooked chicken from a Sunday roast instead of the chicken legs, if you've got it. The mashed potato and mustard sauce can be made ahead, and it can be assembled in advance, too. See my mashed potato masterclass on page 237 for the ultimate pie topping.

4 chicken legs, or 4 ready-roasted chicken legs
2 tbsp butter (plus an extra 2 tbsp if using uncooked chicken)
4 leeks, thinly sliced into 5mm-thick rounds and rinsed
100ml good-quality chicken stock
100g Cheddar cheese, grated (optional)
sea salt and freshly ground black pepper

FOR THE MASHED POTATO

400g King Edward potatoes (or other floury variety), peeled and cut into large equal-sized chunks
50g butter, melted
75–100ml warm milk
pinch of table salt
2 egg yolks

FOR THE WHOLEGRAIN MUSTARD SAUCE

60g butter
60g plain flour
300ml milk
200ml good-quality chicken stock
1 tbsp Dijon mustard
2 tbsp wholegrain mustard

1. Preheat the oven to 220°C/200°C fan/gas 7.

2. If using uncooked chicken legs, lay a sheet of foil on your work surface. Place the chicken legs, 2 tablespoons of the butter and a generous pinch of salt and pepper on top then gather the foil around it. Place the package on a baking tray and bake for 25–30 minutes. Remove from the oven and allow to cool in the foil for 20 minutes, then unwrap and roughly shred the chicken, discarding the bones and skin. If you are using ready-roasted chicken legs, do the same with those.

3. Melt the remaining butter in a large frying pan, add the leeks, season generously with salt and pepper and cook for about 5 minutes over medium heat until they start to wilt, then add the chicken stock and simmer for 3–4 minutes until the leeks are almost cooked through.

4. Put the potatoes for the mash in a saucepan of salted water and bring to the boil. Simmer for around 20 minutes, until tender, then drain well, return to the pan off the heat and mash with the melted butter and milk until smooth. Add the table salt and egg yolks and mix well.

5. To make the wholegrain mustard sauce, melt the butter in a medium saucepan and when it starts bubbling whisk in the flour. Cook for 30 seconds, stirring, then gradually whisk in the milk and stock, a little at a time. When all the milk and stock have been added, bring the sauce to a gentle simmer and cook for 5 minutes, whisking regularly to prevent it catching on the bottom of the pan. Remove from the heat, add both mustards and season with sea salt. Add the chicken and leeks and mix well.

6. Pour the chicken and leek mix into a casserole dish or deep pie dish (about 26cm). Top with the mashed potato, smoothing it over, then fluff up the surface with a fork, and sprinkle over the grated cheese (if using). Bake in the oven for 15–20 minutes until lightly golden on top and bubbling, remove from the oven and serve.

Chicken, Split Pea and Kale Curry

SERVES: 4 | PREP TIME: 15 MINUTES | COOKING TIME: 55 MINUTES

There often seems to be a jar of split peas lurking in the back of store cupboards, and this is a great recipe to get the most out of them. They add a lovely richness to this nutritious curry, and also help bulk it out. I prefer to use chicken legs or thighs in a curry, rather than chicken breast, as the fat content makes them a bit more flavoursome, and stops them drying out as chicken breasts can tend to do.

4 tbsp vegetable oil

4 boneless, skinless chicken thighs, diced into large chunks

200g kale, thick stems removed and leaves roughly chopped

180g yellow split peas, rinsed well under cold running water

1 x 400ml tin coconut milk

sea salt

steamed rice, to serve

FOR THE SPICE BASE

2 onions, halved and sliced

3 garlic cloves, peeled and finely grated (use a Microplane if you have one)

4cm piece of fresh ginger, peeled and finely grated (use a Microplane if you have one)

8cm piece of fresh turmeric, peeled and finely grated (or 1 tbsp ground turmeric)

1 green chilli, finely diced

2 bay leaves

12 green cardamom pods, bashed well

1 tsp ground cinnamon

1 tbsp cumin seeds

1 tbsp black mustard seeds

1. Heat half the vegetable oil in a large frying pan over medium-high heat. Season the chicken pieces with salt and pepper then fry them in the hot oil for around 5 minutes. Once browned, but not cooked through, remove them from the pan and set aside. Return the pan to the heat and turn the heat up to high. Add the kale and fry for 3–4 minutes until browned, then set aside.

2. Heat the remaining vegetable oil in a large saucepan over medium heat. Add all the ingredients for the spice base, season with a little salt and cook for 5 minutes, until fragrant.

3. Add 300ml warm water and the split peas, stirring well. Cover with a lid and simmer gently over low heat for 20 minutes, stirring regularly.

4. Mix in the coconut milk then add the browned chicken and simmer for a further 15 minutes, covered.

5. Mix in the kale and cook for a further 5 minutes, covered.

6. Remove from the heat, discard the cardamom pods and bay leaves and serve with steamed rice.

Hasselback Potatoes with Red Wine and Pork Ragu

SERVES: 4 | PREP TIME: 20 MINUTES | COOKING TIME: ABOUT 1½ HOURS

Hasselback potatoes are a firm everyday favourite in my household. They are pretty quick to prepare, and they are delicious – crispy on the outside and soft in the centre. They go very well with this pork ragu, which can be made ahead and chilled or frozen. The ragu can also be used as a very tasty pasta sauce, or in a lasagne, ready for a speedy midweek meal.

850g small–medium baking potatoes
40g butter, melted
100g Cheddar cheese, grated

FOR THE RAGU
1 tbsp vegetable oil
300g minced pork
6 smoked bacon rashers, finely chopped
1 onion, chopped
1 garlic clove, finely grated
2 carrots, finely diced
300ml red wine
1 × 400g tin chopped tomatoes
2 tbsp tomato purée
1 tbsp sweet smoked paprika
1 tbsp Worcestershire sauce
1 tbsp Dijon mustard
200ml good-quality beef or chicken stock
1 bay leaf
sea salt and freshly ground black pepper

1. To make the ragu, heat the oil in a large saucepan over medium-high heat. Add the minced pork and bacon and fry for 7–9 minutes, until brown all over, breaking up any clumps of meat with a wooden spoon. Stir in the onion, garlic and carrots and continue to fry for another 10 minutes until the onion softens. Season with salt and pepper, pour in the wine and bring to the boil, to allow the wine to reduce completely. Stir in the tomatoes, tomato purée, smoked paprika, Worcestershire sauce, mustard, stock and bay leaf. Bring to a simmer, cover and cook gently over low heat for up to 1 hour. Once cooked, remove from the heat, taste and add a little more seasoning if you like, and remove the bay leaf.

2. Preheat the oven to 220°C/200°C fan/gas 7.

3. Place a potato on your chopping board. Take 2 wooden spoons and line the handles up with the potato – one in front and one behind. Slice into the potato, making cuts 4mm apart, all the way along the potato, ensuring your knife hits the spoon handles (thus preventing you from cutting all the way through). Repeat with the remaining potatoes.

4. Place the cut potatoes in a roasting dish and brush them liberally with the melted butter. Season well with salt and pepper and bake in the oven for 45–50 minutes, until the potatoes are crispy on the outside and soft in the centre.

5. Spoon the ragu over the potatoes, top with the grated cheese, and return to the oven for 10 minutes until bubbling. Remove from the oven and serve with a vegetable side dish.

MARCUS' TIP:
When Jersey Royals are in season do try using them for this recipe. Grown in Jersey, fertilised with seaweed, they have a lovely earthy, mineral flavour.

Rump Steak with Green Sauce and Beer-braised Onions

SERVES: 4 | PREP TIME: 15 MINUTES | COOKING TIME: ABOUT 20 MINUTES

Rump steak is full of flavour, and if you source your meat from a great supplier, you will enjoy it all the more. When cooking steak, you will always get the best result from a very hot pan or griddle pan. Open all your windows before cooking, and be prepared to turn the smoke alarm off – it is all worth it for a well-cooked steak (see my masterclass on page 131). The green sauce is a favourite of mine.

2 tbsp vegetable oil
4 rump steaks (around 250g each) (brined
   for 2 hours if you wish – use 1 quantity
   of the brine on page 242)
20g butter, cubed
sea salt and freshly ground black pepper

FOR THE BEER-BRAISED ONIONS

2 tbsp vegetable oil
4 onions, halved crossways
25g butter
125ml beer (not too bitter)

FOR THE GREEN SAUCE

2 heaped tbsp finely chopped tarragon
   leaves
2 heaped tbsp finely chopped flat-leaf
   parsley leaves
2 heaped tbsp finely chopped oregano
   leaves
1 tsp drained capers in brine, plus extra
   to serve
1 small onion, finely diced
2 tbsp malt vinegar
125ml extra virgin olive oil

1. Start with the onions. You will need a frying pan that will snugly fit 8 onion halves, cut-side down. Heat the oil in the pan over high heat. Season the oil with salt then place the onions, cut-side down, in the pan. Brown well for 8–12 minutes then add the butter, followed by the beer. Cover, turn down the heat to a simmer and cook for 15–20 minutes, until the onions are soft to the touch. Turn off the heat and set aside (uncovered).

2. To make the green sauce, put all of the ingredients in a food processor or blender and pulse until you have a chunky sauce.

3. Bring the steak to room temperature (rinsing off the brine and patting dry with kitchen paper, if steaks were brined). To cook the steak, heat half of the oil in a griddle pan or heavy-based frying pan over high heat. When smoking, season 2 of the steaks with salt and pepper and place them in the hot oil. Sear for 1–2 minutes until golden brown then turn over and sear the other side for a further 1–2 minutes. Add half of the butter and when it melts, tilt the pan towards you and spoon the butter over the steaks continuously, turning them over once during the process. Cook the steaks for 1–2 minutes in the butter (the cooking time will depend on the thickness of the steak, and the doneness you like it cooked to) then remove and keep somewhere warm, covered with foil. Repeat with the remaining 2 steaks. Pour the pan juices over the steaks and serve with the onions and green sauce, plus a few capers, if using.

Pancetta and Mushroom Pasta Bake

SERVES: 4 | PREP TIME: 15 MINUTES | COOKING TIME: 1¼ HOURS

It is hard to beat a delicious bacon and mushroom pasta dish. Here, it is slightly tweaked, using pancetta instead of bacon and creating a rich mushroom sauce as well as using sautéed mushrooms. I have also added spinach, to provide the meal with a few more nutrients. I recommend making the mushroom sauce ahead of time. It will keep in the fridge for up to 3 days, meaning it takes less time to prepare this weeknight supper.

1 tbsp vegetable oil
200g smoked pancetta, diced
250g chestnut or button mushrooms,
   thinly sliced
200g baby leaf spinach
½ bunch of flat-leaf parsley, leaves
   chopped
400g fresh penne pasta or 300g dried
100g Cheddar cheese, grated
sea salt and freshly ground black pepper

FOR THE MUSHROOM SAUCE
25g butter
1 onion, sliced
1 garlic clove, crushed
¼ bunch of thyme
250g field (flat) mushrooms, sliced
300ml good-quality chicken or vegetable
   stock
200ml milk

MARCUS' TIP:
Make a double batch of the mushroom sauce and freeze half of it. It is a versatile recipe – add more stock and you have a soup, or use it as is for a tasty sauce to accompany chicken or fish dishes.

1. To make the mushroom sauce, melt the butter in a large, wide saucepan over medium heat until it begins to froth. Add the onion, garlic and thyme, season well with salt and pepper and cook for 20–25 minutes, stirring frequently, until the onion is golden and caramelised. Increase the heat to medium-high, add the mushrooms and cook for 10–15 minutes, until any liquid from the mushrooms has almost evaporated. Add the stock and milk and simmer gently for 10 minutes. Remove from the heat and discard the thyme stalks. Purée the sauce in a blender or food processor until smooth, taste and add a little more seasoning, if you like.

2. Heat the vegetable oil in a large frying pan over high heat, add the pancetta and let it brown, then turn down the heat to medium and cook for another 5 minutes, to render some of the fat from the pancetta. Using a slotted spoon, transfer the cooked pancetta to the mushroom sauce. Return the pan to high heat and when hot, add the mushrooms, seasoning them well. Fry until golden and all the liquid has evaporated, then add the entire contents of the pan to the mushroom sauce. If you're making the sauce ahead of time, let it cool, then chill until required.

3. Preheat the oven to 230°C/210°C fan/gas 8.

4. Bring a large pan of salted water to the boil and blanch the spinach for 1 minute. Remove with a slotted spoon, refresh under cold running water and drain well. Squeeze out the excess moisture from the leaves and roughly chop. Add these to the mushroom sauce. Finish the sauce with the chopped parsley.

5. Cook the penne in the pan of water you cooked the spinach in, a minute or two less than the packet instructions state. Drain and mix into the mushroom sauce. Place the pasta and mushroom mixture in a large ovenproof dish (about 20 x 30cm) and cover with the grated cheese and a generous grinding of black pepper. Bake in the oven for 10–15 minutes until the cheese has melted and the pasta bake is bubbling. Remove from the oven and serve.

Pork Chops with Green Olives, Baked Orange and Fennel

SERVES: 4 | PREP TIME: 15 MINUTES, PLUS BRINING AND COOLING
COOKING TIME: ABOUT 45 MINUTES

I really enjoy the combination of salty green olives, sweet orange and crunchy fennel. It makes for a great salad on its own, but here, juicy pork chops are a welcome addition. As in my last book, *New Classics*, I do tend to brine quite a lot of my meat; it is a worthwhile exercise and just takes a little forward planning to achieve. Baked orange is also a flavour you must try – the baking minimises the bitterness of the pith and adds a delicious bittersweet, molasses-like flavour, and a scent of fruitiness to the dressing. I suggest baking the orange in advance so it is ready to go on the day.

1 orange
4 large pork chops (about 900g in total), (brined for 2 hours if you wish – use 1 quantity of the brine on page 242)
2 tbsp vegetable oil
100g pitted Gordal olives, sliced
1 large fennel bulb, thinly sliced
sea salt

FOR THE DRESSING
100ml extra virgin olive oil
2 tbsp caper brine
1 tbsp white wine vinegar
2 tbsp wholegrain mustard
1 tbsp honey

1. Preheat the oven to 220°C/200°C fan/gas 7.

2. Put the whole orange in an ovenproof dish and place in the oven for 25–30 minutes, until golden on the outside. Remove, leave to cool then refrigerate until fully chilled. When cool, cut the orange in half then finely dice.

3. Bring the pork chops to room temperature. Heat the vegetable oil in a griddle pan or frying pan over high heat. Rinse the pork chops under cold running water (if you brined them) and pat them dry with kitchen paper. When the oil is almost smoking, add the chops and fry them for about 3 minutes on each side, in batches if necessary. Place the seared chops on a roasting tray and transfer to the oven to cook for a further 6 minutes. Remove and allow to rest, covered loosely with foil, for 5 minutes.

4. Combine the dressing ingredients and the finely diced baked orange in a jug and blend using a stick blender, until a chunky dressing is formed. Season to taste.

5. Mix the olives and sliced fennel together in a bowl, season well with salt and pepper and dress with the dressing. Serve with the pork chops.

Beef, Asparagus, Cashew and Miso Stir-fry

SERVES: 4 | PREP TIME: 10 MINUTES | COOKING TIME: ABOUT 10 MINUTES

A stir-fry is such a great meal. When cooked properly, the meat should be tender and the vegetables still crunchy. I use lettuce in this recipe as I really like the flavour it takes on when lightly grilled. It retains its bite in the centre and gives a fresh texture to the dish. I am a big fan of cashew nuts too, and they give this recipe a lovely richness. These are great flavours in a stir-fry.

100g cashew nuts

2 tbsp vegetable oil

600g steak (I prefer sirloin but rump is also good), cut into 5mm-thick strips

2 tsp tamari or dark soy sauce

2 baby gem lettuces, quartered lengthways

1 tbsp white miso paste

2 tbsp toasted sesame oil

2 onions, thinly sliced

1 garlic clove, finely grated

1 green chilli, thinly sliced

500g asparagus, tough ends trimmed and tender spears sliced in half diagonally

½ bunch of coriander leaves (optional), to garnish

steamed white rice, or rice noodles, to serve

1. Heat a large frying pan or wok over very high heat. Toss in the cashews and stir-fry them in the dry pan for a minute or two until golden brown, then tip out onto a plate.

2. Add half of the vegetable oil and when the oil begins to smoke, add half of the steak and cook it very quickly, for about 30 seconds. Add half the tamari or soy sauce and cook for a further 30 seconds. Transfer the beef from the pan to a plate, place the pan back over the heat and repeat the process with the remaining oil, steak and tamari or soy, transferring the meat to the plate with the rest of the steak when it's seared. While the pan is hot, sear the lettuce briefly, in batches, then remove and set aside.

3. Clean the pan and place it back over the heat. Mix the miso paste and sesame oil with 2 tablespoons of water. Add half the mixture to the pan and place over high heat. Add the onions, garlic and chilli and cook for 3–4 minutes until soft. Add another tablespoon of water to the pan then add the asparagus. Cover the pan and cook for 2 minutes. Remove the cover and add the steak, any resting juices, the seared lettuce and the remaining miso sauce. Cook for 1 minute then stir in the toasted cashews and coriander (if using).

4. Serve the stir-fry with steamed white rice or rice noodles.

Lamb Chops with Minted Orzo and Pea Salad

SERVES: 4 | PREP TIME: 10 MINUTES, PLUS COOLING
COOKING TIME: ABOUT 25 MINUTES

Lamb, mint and peas! A great, classic English combination that works so well – it brings back childhood for me. This recipe makes a great summer supper, and the salad on its own can also make a really delicious lunch – I just add a little crumbled feta and some toasted pine nuts.

25g butter

1 onion, finely diced

1 red chilli, deseeded and finely chopped

200g frozen peas, defrosted

250g orzo pasta

8 lamb loin chops (brined for 2 hours if you wish – use 1 quantity of the brine on page 242)

sea salt and freshly ground black pepper

FOR THE FRESH MINT DRESSING

6 tbsp malt vinegar

2 tsp caster sugar

1 red onion, thinly sliced

4 tbsp olive oil, plus extra for brushing

1 bunch of mint, leaves picked and finely chopped

1. To make the fresh mint dressing, heat the malt vinegar in a small saucepan over medium heat, add the sugar and stir to dissolve. Remove the pan from the heat and add the red onion. Set aside until cool. When cool, prepare a large bowl of iced water. Place the vinegar and red onion, olive oil and mint leaves in a small food processor or blender and blitz until smooth. Place in a bowl over the bowl of iced water and whisk until completely cold, to retain the green colour.

2. Heat the butter in a medium saucepan over medium heat. When hot, add the diced onion and chilli. Season well and cook for around 10 minutes until soft but not coloured, then add the peas and cook for 1 minute. Transfer to a food processor or blender and pulse lightly, to retain the texture.

3. Remove the lamb chops from the fridge and let them come to room temperature (rinsing off the brine and patting dry with kitchen paper, if lamb was brined). Bring a medium-large saucepan of salted water to the boil. Cook the orzo pasta according to the packet instructions, then rinse under cold running water until cool and drain well.

4. Heat a griddle pan over high heat until very hot. Brush the lamb chops all over with a little olive oil and season with salt and pepper on both sides. Sit the chops fat-side down on the griddle, leaning them up against each other for support. Cook for 4–5 minutes until the fat renders and becomes crisp, then lay the chops flat on their sides and cook for a further 3–5 minutes on each side, basting them with the rendered fat. Remove the chops from the pan and set aside to rest for 5 minutes. You may have to cook the lamb chops in batches.

5. Combine the orzo with the peas and half of the mint dressing. Season well with salt and pepper.

6. Serve the chops with the remaining mint dressing drizzled over the top, and the orzo salad on the side.

Lamb Meatballs with Harissa and Sour Cream

SERVES: 4 | PREP TIME: ABOUT 15 MINUTES
COOKING TIME: ABOUT 45 MINUTES

Lamb mince is packed full of flavour and richness, so I always have a packet on hand in the freezer for a quick meal. In summer, I like to serve these meatballs stuffed into pita breads or in tortilla wraps, with some finely shredded iceberg lettuce. In winter, they work well with brown rice, couscous or some good old mashed potato. Both the meatballs and sauce can be made ahead.

2 tbsp vegetable oil
2 tbsp rose harissa paste
150g sour cream
¼ bunch of coriander, leaves chopped

FOR THE MEATBALLS

600g minced lamb
1 onion, finely diced
4 tbsp tomato ketchup
2 tbsp drained capers in brine, chopped
1 tbsp Dijon mustard
2 tbsp Worcestershire sauce
1 bunch of flat-leaf parsley, leaves finely chopped
50g dried breadcrumbs
½ tsp table salt
1 egg, beaten

FOR THE TOMATO SAUCE

1 tbsp vegetable oil
1 red onion, finely diced
½ tsp table salt
2 tbsp white wine vinegar
2 tbsp tomato purée
400g tomato passata

1. To make the meatballs, combine all the ingredients in a bowl. Divide the mix into 20 pieces and roll into balls.

2. To make the tomato sauce, heat the vegetable oil in a medium saucepan over medium heat, add the diced red onion and salt and cook for about 10 minutes until soft. Add the vinegar and cook until it has evaporated, then mix in the tomato purée and passata and simmer gently for 10 minutes.

3. Preheat the oven to 200°C/180°C fan/gas 6.

4. Heat the 2 tablespoons of vegetable oil in a large frying pan over medium-high heat. Add the meatballs and brown them for 5–7 minutes (in batches, so you don't overcrowd the pan). Place the meatballs in a 20cm square baking dish that fits all the meatballs snugly, cover with the tomato sauce and bake for 15 minutes until bubbling.

5. Mix the harissa paste, sour cream and coriander together and spoon the mixture over the meatballs when they come out of the oven.

MARCUS' TIP:
You will notice tomato ketchup in a few mince recipes, which may surprise you. The tomatoes in ketchup add sweetness, a little acidity and richness. Used in moderation (it has a lot of sugar), it's a simple way to add flavour.

Potato, Thyme and Cheese Croquettes

Carrot Fritters with Pickle Juice Emulsion and Carrot Salad

Homemade Ricotta, Radicchio, Orange and Dill Salad

Panzanella

Leftovers Frittata with Piquant Fruit Chutney

Not-So-Ordinary Tomato Sauce

Pizza Base

Cauliflower and Yellow Split Pea Curry

Fridge Gazpacho

Quick Vegetable Pickle

Fruit Bowl Compote

Winter Warmer Soup

Baked Citrus and Polenta Cake

Sticky Banana Pudding with Rosemary Sauce
and Homemade Crème Fraîche

Waste Not, Want Not

Waste Not, Want Not

My dad's business was selling basic fruit and potatoes – farmed produce grown by hardworking people. We bought it, looked after it and sold it. This chapter comes directly from my upbringing, in which waste was not allowed. This approach made me stand out from the crowd in professional kitchens. It's about respecting ingredients and having a good understanding of their value. The process is the same – it's just dressed up in a slightly different way in a professional kitchen. It's crucial in the world in which we live that we only buy what we need, and that we cherish what we purchase. We mustn't waste food or throw it away, and we shouldn't look at it as if it's cheap. If you regard produce as if someone's made it and use it well, you can save a lot of money and really manage your spending.

Potato, Thyme and Cheese Croquettes

SERVES: 6–8 AS A STARTER OR SIDE | PREP TIME: 40 MINUTES, PLUS COOLING AND CHILLING | COOKING TIME: ABOUT 1 HOUR

This is a great recipe for using up those old, soft potatoes lying in the bottom of your fridge or cupboard. And those small end pieces of cheese in the fridge, including blue cheese or soft cheese, can be used here too, for extra flavour.

450g potatoes
15g butter
1 onion, finely diced
1 tbsp thyme leaves, picked
50g cheese, grated
vegetable oil, for deep-frying
sea salt and freshly ground black pepper

FOR THE CHEESE SAUCE
250ml milk
25g butter
25g plain flour
100g cheese of choice, grated
1 tsp Dijon mustard
2 tbsp Worcestershire sauce

FOR THE CRUMB
40g plain flour, seasoned with salt and
   pepper
2 eggs, beaten
100g dried breadcrumbs (panko or
   homemade from stale bread)

MARCUS' TIP:
Don't discard your potato peelings. Toss them with a teaspoon of olive oil, then bake in an oven preheated to 200°C/180°C fan/gas 6 for 8–12 minutes and serve with harissa mayo.

1. Preheat the oven to 200°C/180°C fan/gas 6.

2. Scrub the potatoes, pierce them with a fork and place them on a baking tray. Bake in the oven for 35–40 minutes until soft. Slice open, in a cross formation, to allow the steam to escape. When cool enough to handle, scoop out the flesh and pass it through a sieve, mouli or potato ricer into a bowl. Set aside.

3. While the potatoes are baking, make the cheese sauce. Put the milk in a small saucepan. Gently bring to the boil over low heat. Melt the butter in a small saucepan and add the flour and a pinch each of salt and pepper. Cook, stirring, over low heat for about 1 minute (avoid letting it brown). Add a ladle of the hot milk and stir to combine. Continue adding the milk a bit at a time until you have a thick sauce. Bring to a simmer, then mix in the cheese, mustard and Worcestershire sauce. Stir until melted. Cover and remove from the heat.

4. Heat the 15g of butter in a frying pan over medium heat. Add the onion and cook for about 10 minutes, until soft but not coloured. Add the thyme, then add to the sauce with the grated cheese. Transfer to a large bowl. Add the mashed potato and mix well. Chill for 3 hours until firm. Using wet hands, form into balls, roughly 20g each, and chill for 20 minutes.

5. While the croquettes are in the fridge, pour enough vegetable oil into a deep saucepan or deep-fat fryer to come up to about 5cm and place over medium heat. If using a deep-fat fryer or if you have a thermometer, heat the oil to 170°C. If not, to check the oil is at the right temperature, drop a 2–3cm cube of bread into the hot oil – it should turn golden and crisp in 1 minute.

6. While the oil heats, put the crumb ingredients in 3 bowls. Coat the croquettes in the flour, then the egg, then a generous coating of crumbs. Chill (on a tray) for 10 minutes.

7. Carefully lower a batch of croquettes into the hot oil and fry for 4 minutes, or until they rise to the surface with a hissing sound. Lift out carefully with a slotted spoon, drain on kitchen paper and serve hot. Repeat with the remaining croquettes.

Carrot Fritters with Pickle Juice Emulsion and Carrot Salad

SERVES: 4 | PREP TIME: 30 MINUTES | COOKING TIME: 25 MINUTES

Carrots are a versatile ingredient in so many recipes, but are sometimes overlooked as an ingredient in their own right. I always have some in the fridge so I thought it would be good to create a recipe for when they are starting to lose their crispness. And I am sure you all have a jar of pickles in the fridge which is 90 per cent pickle juice and 10 per cent pickle, and the juice usually gets thrown down the sink. But this can be used in many ways – here it is used to create a sauce for the fritters. Serve this as a main course for a summer lunch, with some spelt, wild rice or lentils.

1kg carrots, peeled
sea salt and freshly ground black pepper

FOR THE FRITTERS
½ tsp table salt
4 spring onions, trimmed and thinly sliced
½ tsp caraway seeds, finely crushed
2 eggs
2 tbsp olive oil
6 tbsp plain flour
½ tsp baking powder
vegetable oil, for frying

FOR THE PICKLE JUICE EMULSION
50ml pickle juice, strained
30g butter, cubed

FOR THE CARROT SALAD
½ bunch coriander, leaves chopped
2 tbsp chopped toasted almonds (see page 126 for method)
1 tsp wholegrain mustard

MARCUS' TIP:
As you may have noticed, I use a lot of mustard to add flavour in my recipes. I always have Dijon, English and wholegrain mustards in my fridge.

1. Set aside 1 large carrot. Coarsely grate the remaining (roughly 800g) carrots. Place them in a colander, sprinkle with the table salt and leave for 10 minutes.

2. Thinly slice (using a peeler) or spiralise the remaining carrot and set aside.

3. Squeeze out and reserve all the juice from the grated carrots, then place the carrots in a large mixing bowl. Add half the spring onions, the caraway seeds, eggs and 2 tablespoons of olive oil. Mix and add a generous grind of pepper. Combine the flour and baking powder and fold into the wet ingredients.

4. Put enough vegetable oil into a large non-stick frying pan to cover the base. Place over medium heat. When hot, put a small spoonful of the fritter mix in the pan. Brown on each side then taste and add more salt if needed. Add heaped tablespoons of the mixture to the pan, pressing them down with the back of a spoon to make fritters about 5mm thick. Fry for 4–5 minutes on each side, until browned a little, the edges are crisped and they are cooked through. Repeat with the rest of the fritter mix. Drain on kitchen paper and keep warm.

5. Place the pickle juice in a small saucepan and bring to a simmer. Add the butter, cube by cube, and swirl the pan until the butter has combined with the pickle juice to create a silky sauce.

6. Mix the sliced or spiralised carrot with the coriander, toasted almonds and remaining spring onions, and season with salt. Mix the carrot juice from step 3 with the wholegrain mustard and mix through the salad.

7. Serve the warm fritters with a small spoonful of the emulsion and the carrot salad.

Homemade Ricotta, Radicchio, Orange and Dill Salad

SERVES: 4 | PREP TIME: 15 MINUTES, PLUS CHILLING
COOKING TIME: ABOUT 10 MINUTES

Homemade ricotta cheese is very simple to make, and is a great way to use up any whole milk that is nearing its use-by date. It's also really good fun to prepare it under the watchful eyes of young children – it's fascinating to see the milk split, and a little bit magical. If you want it a touch creamier, add a splash of cream. The slightly sour whey is also an incredibly useful by-product. In this recipe I reduce it down and use it in the salad dressing, though you can also chill it then use it in baking and bread-making. This is not a recipe for when you're in a rush, so save it for the weekend. You can of course get your ricotta from the supermarket instead, but I urge you to give this technique a go.

2 oranges, zest grated then fruit peeled
   and segmented
½ tbsp wholegrain mustard
1 gherkin, diced
25ml olive oil
1 large head of radicchio, separated into
   leaves
¼ bunch of dill, fronds picked
sea salt and freshly ground black pepper

FOR THE RICOTTA
1 litre whole milk
juice of 1 lemon, grated zest of ½
1 tsp cider vinegar

1. Pour the milk for the ricotta into a large saucepan and bring to the boil, stirring regularly to stop it catching on the bottom. Boil for 1 minute then whisk in the lemon juice and vinegar. Turn down the heat to low. Allow to almost simmer and you should see the curds begin to form after a minute or two. Stir the milk gently and leave for another 5 minutes. Strain the ricotta through a fine sieve, keeping the whey. Leave to strain for 3 minutes, then transfer to a mixing bowl. Add the lemon zest, season to taste with salt and pepper and whisk well. Cover, refrigerate and use within 3 days.

2. Pour the whey into a medium saucepan and bring to a rapid simmer. Simmer for 10–20 minutes until you have a viscous liquid of about 100ml.

3. Pour half of the reduced whey into a mixing bowl (refrigerate the other 50ml to use another time). Whisk in the orange zest, wholegrain mustard, gherkin and olive oil. Season with salt and pepper.

4. To assemble the salad, lay the radicchio leaves on a serving platter. Drizzle with the dressing then dollop the ricotta around the leaves. Scatter the orange segments over the top and finish with the dill fronds.

MARCUS' TIP:
Dill can sometimes be a forgotten herb but it adds so much flavour to salads, fish dishes and pasta. It grows very easily too.

Panzanella

SERVES: 4 | PREP TIME: 15 MINUTES, PLUS STRAINING AND SOAKING
COOKING TIME: 10 MINUTES

Panzanella, a Tuscan-style stale bread and tomato salad, is like a grab-and-go – we've all got bread going stale somewhere, we've all got too many tomatoes somewhere, on the verge of being overripe. And this recipe injects life into them, reviving something that's almost on its way to the bin. This recipe is just a framework, so if there are other ingredients in your fridge that would work well, such as peppers (in a jar or fresh), pickled onions or baby gem lettuce, then go ahead and add them, as this chapter is all about trying to prevent waste.

300g fresh or stale bread, cut into thick slices
6 medium overripe tomatoes
100ml tomato juice from a carton
2 garlic cloves, finely grated
4 tbsp balsamic vinegar
100ml olive oil
1 tsp Dijon mustard
2 tbsp capers in brine, plus 1 tsp caper brine
1 red onion, thinly sliced
50g pitted kalamata olives, roughly chopped
½ bunch of basil, leaves roughly chopped
½ bunch of flat-leaf parsley, leaves roughly chopped
sea salt and freshly ground black pepper

1. If you're using fresh bread, preheat the oven to 170°C/150°C fan/gas 4, line a baking tray with baking parchment and lay out the bread slices in one layer. Bake for 10 minutes then remove from the oven.

2. While the bread is baking, cut the tomatoes into small wedges. Toss them in salt then place them in a colander set over a bowl. Set aside for 20 minutes, reserving the juice.

3. Place the tomatoes in a large bowl.

4. Add the tomato juice, the garlic, 2 tablespoons of the balsamic vinegar and 50ml of the olive oil to the fresh tomato juice in the bowl. Mix together and season well with salt and pepper.

5. Cut the bread into 2cm dice and place in a shallow dish large enough to fit the bread in a single layer. Pour the tomato juice mix over the top and leave to sit for 20 minutes.

6. Mix the remaining balsamic vinegar and olive oil together. Add the mustard and caper brine and season with salt and pepper.

7. Add the soaked bread, red onion, capers, olives and herbs to the tomatoes and gently mix together with the dressing. Serve immediately.

MARCUS' TIP:
Eating stale bread might not sound so delicious, but marinating it actually brings it back to life. It's stale because it's gone dry, so you're just rehydrating it. Obviously, don't use mouldy bread!

Leftovers Frittata with Piquant Fruit Chutney

SERVES: 4 | PREP TIME: 15 MINUTES | COOKING TIME: ABOUT 50 MINUTES

This makes a quick and easy supper – perfect for a Sunday night if you have leftovers from the weekend. The recipe is adaptable, so experiment with what you have – courgette, onions, sweet potato, broccoli and cauliflower all work well – just avoid any raw vegetables that have a high water content, as this will prevent the frittata from setting. The speedy fruit chutney can be made any time you have a glut of ripe or overripe fruit in your fruit bowl (such as apples, quince, plums, rhubarb or peaches), then it can be stored in the fridge for up to 4 weeks (unopened). Generally, chutneys tend to get cooked for hours, but with this one the liquids are reduced, then the fresh ingredients are folded into it, which keeps the flavours fresh.

FOR THE FRUIT CHUTNEY

½ tsp coriander seeds
½ tsp fennel seeds
1 clove
2 bay leaves
40ml cider vinegar
2 tbsp soft dark brown sugar
1 garlic clove, crushed
1 onion, finely diced
200g fruit, peeled, cored, stoned and diced

FOR THE FRITTATA

25g butter
2 onions, thinly sliced
2 tbsp olive oil
500g cooked vegetables, cut into evenly
    sized chunks
80g Gruyère or Cheddar cheese, grated
8 eggs
sea salt and freshly ground black pepper

MARCUS' TIP:
Frittata is a great addition to a lunchbox. Make one the night before, chill and then cut into portions. It's a good source of protein and vegetables and is delicious cold, too.

1. To make the chutney, start by putting the coriander seeds, fennel seeds and clove in a medium saucepan over medium heat. Toast until fragrant then transfer to a spice grinder or pestle and mortar and grind. Return the ground spices to the saucepan and add the other ingredients. Place over low heat and cook for 5 minutes, until the fruit begins to soften, then increase the heat to medium and simmer for 15–20 minutes, stirring regularly and adding a splash of water (2–3 tablespoons) if needed. Remove the bay leaves then turn off the heat and leave the chutney to sit for a further 15 minutes. Season to taste with salt and pepper.

2. For the frittata, preheat the oven to 190°C/170°C fan/gas 5.

3. While the chutney is cooking, place a medium, ovenproof frying pan (about 20cm) on medium heat. Add the butter and, when melted, add the onions and season well with salt and pepper. Cook for 20–25 minutes until the onions are deeply golden then remove from the pan. Add the olive oil to the pan and when hot, add the leftover vegetables. Heat for about 5 minutes until warmed through, then add the onions back to the pan. Mix well and add the cheese.

4. Beat the eggs in a bowl, season with salt and pepper then pour into the pan. Stir once then place the entire pan in the oven. Bake for about 15 minutes, until the egg is just set in the centre.

5. Serve hot, or cold, with the fruit chutney and a green salad.

Not-So-Ordinary Tomato Sauce

MAKES: 1.5KG | PREP TIME: 15 MINUTES | COOKING TIME: ABOUT 45 MINUTES

Homemade tomato sauce is a great thing to have portioned up and ready to go in the freezer, so you can just defrost it when required. And you don't have to spend hours and hours making it. This can be used for pasta, as a base for pizza, in Bolognese sauces or ragus, hotpots and many more dishes. It also contains some hidden vegetables, for added nutrition.

2 tbsp vegetable oil
4 onions, thinly sliced
2 garlic cloves, finely grated
1 carrot, peeled and grated (about 110g)
1 courgette, grated (about 180g)
½ sweet potato, peeled and grated
  (about 165g)
200ml vegetable stock
2 tbsp tomato paste
2 x 400g tins chopped tomatoes
2 tbsp balsamic vinegar
1 sprig of rosemary
2 bay leaves
sea salt and freshly ground black pepper

1. Heat the vegetable oil in a large saucepan over medium-high heat. Add the onions, season with salt and cook for 15–20 minutes until lightly golden. Add the garlic and cook until soft, then add the carrot, courgette, sweet potato and vegetable stock and cook for a further 5 minutes over medium heat.

2. Add the remaining ingredients, mix well and turn the heat to medium. Cook gently for a further 20 minutes, stirring regularly. Taste and season if necessary.

3. Remove the rosemary and bay leaves then blend the sauce, using a blender or stick blender, until it reaches your desired consistency.

4. Leave to cool, chill, then freeze in portions.

Pizza Base

MAKES: 4 LARGE PIZZAS | PREP TIME: 15 MINUTES, PLUS RISING
PREP TIME FROM FROZEN: 1½ HOURS DEFROSTING PLUS PROVING

I always find it handy to have these pizza bases ready to go in the freezer. They have had their first prove, so just need to be taken out, topped and left to have their final rise. You can also use these to make a quick and tasty flatbread, with garlic butter, or put one on the barbecue for a quick grilled bread to serve with dinner.

250g strong white bread flour, plus extra for dusting
200g wholemeal flour
7g sachet fast-action dried yeast or easy-bake yeast
½ tsp caster sugar
4 tbsp olive oil, plus extra for greasing
1 tsp table salt

1. Mix the flours, yeast and sugar together in a large bowl.

2. Pour the olive oil and 260–300ml of warm water into a jug. Mix together then add the liquid to the flour, along with the salt. Mix by hand until you have a dough that leaves the sides of the bowl. Turn it out of the bowl and knead it on a lightly floured surface for 7–10 minutes until soft and smooth. Alternatively, make the dough in a stand mixer fitted with a dough hook.

3. Transfer the dough to a clean, lightly oiled bowl, cover with oiled clingfilm and leave in a warm place for about 1 hour, or until the dough has doubled in size.

4. Tip the risen dough out onto a floured work surface. Cut it into 4 equal pieces and roll each piece out to a circle, approximately 25cm in diameter (or cut it into half and roll out 2 larger pizzas). Place each dough circle on a piece of floured baking parchment and dust the top of the dough well with flour. Stack on top of each other on a baking tray. Cover with clingfilm and place in the freezer. When frozen, wrap each one tightly in clingfilm.

5. To defrost: take the dough out of the freezer 1–1½ hours before you want to cook the pizza. Top the dough then leave in a warm place to prove for 20 minutes before baking – see recipe on page 156 for cooking instructions.

MARCUS' TIP:
I use a combination of white and wholemeal flour, as it's a great way to add a little fibre and some vitamins. Most people don't notice when they are smothered in delicious toppings!

Cauliflower and Yellow Split Pea Curry

SERVES: 4 | PREP TIME: 15 MINUTES | COOKING TIME: ABOUT 1 HOUR

Most people throw away cauliflower leaves, but they are a delicious ingredient that can be used in many different ways – try them in salads, soups, stir-fries and curries, like this one. If you prefer a spicier curry, use red chilli instead of green. Cauliflower carries curry flavours really well – the key is to taste the curry as you go, so you can make sure it's not too spicy, not too hot. It sits great on the side of something, or works as a meal in its own right.

1 large head cauliflower, or 2 small heads, with leaves intact
2 tbsp vegetable oil
180g yellow split peas, rinsed well
1 x 400ml tin coconut milk
sea salt
steamed rice or whole grains (such as spelt, barley or freekeh), to serve

FOR THE CURRY BASE

6 cardamom pods, crushed with a pestle and mortar
2 cinnamon sticks
1 tsp cumin seeds
1 tsp coriander seeds
1 tsp yellow or black mustard seeds
2 tbsp vegetable oil
1 onion, finely diced
3 garlic cloves, finely grated
4cm piece of fresh ginger, peeled and finely grated
1 tbsp ground turmeric (or 4cm piece of fresh turmeric, peeled and finely grated)
1 green chilli, finely diced
2 bay leaves
1 bunch of coriander, leaves and stalks separated, leaves chopped and stalks finely chopped

1. Preheat the oven to 220°C/200°C fan/gas 7.

2. Remove the leaves from the cauliflower. Cut the leaves crossways, across the spine, into 1cm-thick strips and set aside. Cut the cauliflower into bite-sized florets.

3. Toss the florets in the vegetable oil and a generous pinch of salt and place in a roasting tray. Roast in the oven for 30–35 minutes until a deep golden colour, tossing them once halfway through the cooking time.

4. While the cauliflower is roasting, place the crushed cardamom pods, cinnamon sticks, cumin, coriander and mustard seeds in a medium saucepan. Place over medium heat and toast until fragrant. Add the vegetable oil then the remaining ingredients, including the coriander stalks (but not the leaves), to the saucepan. Season well with salt and cook for 5 minutes.

5. Add the yellow split peas and 700ml warm water. Stir well then cover and simmer over low heat for 40 minutes, stirring regularly, adding a little more water if the peas have absorbed it. Add the coconut milk and cook for a further 5 minutes.

6. Add the roasted cauliflower florets and the cauliflower leaves, cover and cook for a few minutes until the leaves have wilted. Remove from the heat and scatter over the chopped coriander leaves.

7. Serve with steamed rice or whole grains and your favourite curry accompaniments.

Fridge Gazpacho

SERVES: 8 | PREP TIME: 15 MINUTES, PLUS MARINATING AND CHILLING

Gazpacho is one of my favourite summer lunchtime dishes. It is tasty, refreshing, and a great cooling meal in the heat. To get the most flavour from it, the ingredients need to marinate together for at least 24 hours – the soup will be even better if you leave them for 48 hours. Feel free to substitute any of the summer vegetables or fruit, according to what's available: courgette, lettuce and watermelon all work well, and parsley, tarragon and chives, too.

1kg overripe tomatoes, roughly chopped
1 red or yellow pepper, deseeded and
  roughly chopped
1 red onion, sliced
½ bunch of basil leaves
¼ bunch of dill
1 cucumber, peeled and roughly chopped
1 garlic clove, sliced
1 peach, stoned and roughly chopped,
  or 250g watermelon, rind and seeds
  removed
1 litre tomato juice
4 tbsp Worcestershire sauce
2 tbsp balsamic vinegar
5 dashes of Tabasco
½ tsp table salt
freshly ground black pepper, to taste

1. Put all ingredients in a suitably sized container that will fit in your fridge. Cover and leave to marinate in the fridge for at least 24 hours.

2. Put everything in a blender or food processor and blitz until smooth, adding a little more salt if needed. Refrigerate after blitzing and serve chilled.

Quick Vegetable Pickle

MAKES: 300G PICKLE | PREPARATION TIME: 10 MINUTES, PLUS STANDING TIME
COOKING TIME: UNDER 10 MINUTES

This is a great recipe to have to hand when you have one or two vegetables that you won't have time to use before they spoil. Try the pickling method below with cucumber, carrots, cauliflower, celeriac or lettuce. You can also use this recipe to pickle fruit – some of my favourites are rhubarb, blackberries, peaches and pears. The pickles can be used in sandwiches or salads, and also served with meat and fish.

½ tsp fennel seeds
½ tsp coriander seeds
½ tsp mustard seeds (yellow or black)
150ml white wine vinegar
25g demerara sugar
pinch of sea salt
200–300g vegetables, washed and sliced into even-sized pieces

1. Put the fennel, coriander and mustard seeds in a small saucepan and place over medium heat. Toast until fragrant then add the remaining ingredients (except the vegetables) and bring to a simmer. Simmer until the sugar has dissolved then remove from the heat and allow to stand for 10 minutes.

2. Pour the pickling liquor over the vegetables while it is still warm. Cover and allow to sit for 10 minutes then refrigerate in a sealed glass jar until ready to use (the flavour intensifies the longer the pickle is left).

Fruit Bowl Compote

SERVES: 4 | PREP TIME: 5–10 MINUTES

Having a delicious fruit compote in the freezer ready to go for that warming crumble, fruit tart or even just to serve with pouring cream when you need something sweet, is a satisfying way to preserve seasonal fruits at their best. I have suggested a few of my favourite combinations below. The amount of sweetener you add depends on the amount of natural sugars in the fruits, as well as your own sweet tooth. I find honey is a great alternative to white sugar, so tend to use it frequently.

Spring
Rhubarb and fresh ginger
Strawberry, rhubarb and elderflower

Summer
Apricot and star anise
Peach and raspberry
Cherry and port

Autumn
Plum and apple
Apple and blackberry

Winter
Apple, cinnamon and nutmeg
Quince and orange blossom

BASE RECIPE
800g fruit, prepared and cut to the same size
100g sweetener (such as honey, sugar, maple syrup or fruit cordial)

SPICES
10g dried spice of choice, or
3 cinnamon sticks, or
4 star anise, or
1 nutmeg (finely grated)

LIQUIDS
50ml alcohol of choice
1 tsp orange blossom water, or rose water

1. Place the fruit, sweetener, spices and liquid of choice in a medium saucepan over low heat. Gently heat the fruit until the natural juices begin to come out. Turn up the heat slightly and simmer gently until the fruit is the desired softness.

2. Allow to cool completely then freeze in portions.

Winter Warmer Soup

SERVES: 6 | PREP TIME: 10 MINUTES | COOKING TIME: 3 HOURS 50 MINUTES

This is one of those full-meal-in-a-bowl soups. Do add and leave out ingredients as you, and your fridge or store cupboard, see fit. Barley, freekeh and spelt work well in place of the rice and lentils, and you can use rosemary, parsley or tarragon instead of thyme, if you have them to hand. It freezes well.

1 smoked ham hock (about 1kg)
2 bay leaves
½ bunch of thyme
2 onions, diced
150g brown rice, rinsed
100g green lentils, rinsed
500g winter vegetables such as celeriac, swede, parsnip, Jerusalem artichoke, or squash, diced into 2cm chunks
2 leeks, rinsed and diced (white part only)
sea salt and freshly ground black pepper

1. Place the ham hock in a large saucepan and cover with cold water. Bring to the boil, then drain and rinse the ham under cold running water. Place the ham back in the pan, cover with fresh cold water, and add the bay leaves, thyme and onions. Bring to the boil over high heat, skimming off any scum that rises to the surface with a spoon, then reduce the heat and leave to simmer uncovered for 3 hours, topping up with more water if needed. The ham hock is cooked when you can put a butter knife through it with no resistance.

2. Carefully strain off the liquid into a separate large saucepan. Allow the ham hock to cool slightly then, using two forks or your hands, remove all of the meat, discarding the skin and bones.

3. Add the brown rice to the ham hock cooking liquid with a generous amount of black pepper. Place over high heat and bring to the boil, then reduce the heat to a gentle simmer. Cook for 15 minutes. Add the lentils and the winter vegetables and simmer for a further 20 minutes. Finish with the ham hock meat and leeks, simmering for a further 5–7 minutes. Remove from the heat, taste and add more salt if needed.

4. Serve warm, or chill quickly then portion and freeze.

Baked Citrus and Polenta Cake

SERVES: 8–10 | PREP TIME: 15 MINUTES | COOKING TIME: 1 HOUR, PLUS COOLING

This cake works well with any citrus – old oranges, clementines, grapefruit, lemons and limes – you may have at the bottom of your fruit bowl. Baking them mellows the bitterness of the pith, and intensifies the citrus flavour. This cake is also gluten and dairy free, so a handy one to have in your repertoire.

FOR THE CAKE

300g whole citrus fruit (not just lemons and limes)
150ml light olive oil, plus extra for greasing
2 eggs
200g soft dark brown sugar
200g ground almonds
150g yellow quick-cook polenta
2 tsp baking powder

FOR THE SYRUP

½ tsp fennel seeds
¼ tsp coriander seeds
1 tsp orange blossom water
100ml citrus juice
2–4 tbsp demerara sugar

cream, crème fraîche or thick Greek yoghurt, to serve

1. Preheat the oven to 210°C/190°C fan/gas 7 and grease and line the base of a 23cm springform cake tin.

2. Place the whole citrus fruits on a baking tray or in a roasting tray and bake in the oven for 20–25 minutes until lightly golden, moving them every 8 minutes, so they colour evenly. Remove from the oven and lower the oven to 170°C/150°C fan/gas 4.

3. Place the baked citrus in a blender or food processor with the olive oil and blitz until smooth. Add the eggs and brown sugar and blitz again until combined.

4. Transfer to a mixing bowl, add the ground almonds and mix well. Combine the polenta and baking powder then fold them into the wet ingredients.

5. Transfer the cake batter to the prepared tin and bake in the oven for about 35 minutes, until the cake is just firm in the centre and a skewer inserted into the middle of the cake comes out clean.

6. While the cake is cooling, make the syrup. Place the fennel and coriander seeds in a small saucepan and toast over medium heat until fragrant. Transfer to a spice grinder or pestle and mortar and crush. Place back in the saucepan and add the orange blossom water, citrus juice and 1 tablespoon of the demerara sugar. Place over the heat, bring to the boil and simmer for 5–8 minutes, until syrupy. Taste the syrup and add another tablespoon or two of sugar if you have used more lemon or lime juice. Allow to dissolve, cool for about 5 minutes, then slowly pour the syrup over the top of the cake, ensuring it is soaking in. Sprinkle a half tablespoon of the demerara sugar over the top to finish.

7. Remove the cake from the tin, slice and serve with cream, crème fraîche or Greek yoghurt.

MARCUS' TIP:

Baking recipes that are free from gluten are not as delicate as ones containing gluten. You will see I advise not to over-mix cake batters that contain plain flour, as it causes the gluten to develop and the result is denser than it should be. With gluten-free recipes, however, the risk of over-mixing is minimised, so mix away!

Sticky Banana Pudding with Rosemary Sauce and Homemade Crème Fraîche

MAKES: 8 PUDDINGS | PREP TIME: 25 MINUTES, PLUS 3 DAYS FOR THE CRÈME FRAÎCHE
COOKING TIME: ABOUT 20 MINUTES

Overripe bananas are just made for cooking with. Their flavour is so much more intense, and as the starchiness has converted to a syrupy sugar, they are super-sweet too. The rosemary sauce is really unusual but it works – rosemary has quite a bit of heat and pungency as a herb, and it pairs brilliantly with bananas, complementing their sweetness. Then the homemade crème fraîche cuts through the whole thing. You can make the crème fraîche with any old cream and yoghurt lurking in the fridge. It takes 3 days to make, so start it in advance. Once made, it will keep in the fridge for a few days.

FOR THE CRÈME FRAÎCHE
200ml double cream
2 tbsp plain yoghurt

FOR THE PUDDING
125g soft butter, plus extra for greasing
150g soft dark brown sugar
2 eggs
3 very ripe bananas, mashed well (325g mashed weight)
50g golden syrup
150ml milk
235g plain flour
1 tbsp baking powder
1 tsp bicarbonate of soda

FOR THE SAUCE
70g soft dark brown sugar
25g butter
2 tbsp dark rum
1 sprig of rosemary, leaves picked and finely chopped
½ tsp table salt

1. Start with the créme fraîche. Pour the cream into a mixing bowl and add the yoghurt. Whisk together then transfer to a glass jar. Seal the jar and leave in a warm (but not hot) place for at least 3 days, shaking the jar once a day. After 3 days, open the jar and see how thick it is. If it is still a little runny, leave for another day.

2. For the cake, preheat the oven to 200°C/180°C fan/gas 6. Grease 8 × 175ml ramekins with butter and set on a baking tray.

3. Beat together the butter and sugar in a bowl with an electric whisk or in the bowl of a stand mixer until light and creamy. In a separate bowl, whisk together the eggs, mashed bananas, golden syrup and 50ml of the milk. Add this to the butter and sugar mix and stir until combined. Sift the flour and baking powder together, then fold them into the pudding mix.

4. Heat the remaining 100ml of milk in a saucepan. Bring the milk to the boil then whisk in the bicarbonate of soda. Add this to the pudding mix.

5. Divide the batter evenly among the greased ramekins.

6. Make the sauce. Put the brown sugar in a saucepan with the butter, rum, rosemary leaves, salt and 150ml of boiling water. Bring to a simmer and whisk until the sugar and butter have melted together. Pour over the top of the batter in the ramekins.

7. Bake the puddings (with the ramekins sitting on the baking tray) for 13–15 minutes until cooked through. Turn out directly onto serving bowls and serve with a large dollop of the homemade crème fraîche.

Croque Monsieur

Smoked Salmon and Garden Herb Omelette

Chop Chop Salad

Prawn, Tomato and Chilli Linguine

Chicken Schnitzel with Celeriac Remoulade and a Fried Egg

Butter-roasted Cauliflower with Capers and Parsley

Barnsley Chop, Roasted Fennel and Black Olive Tapenade

Sirloin Steak with Brandy Sauce and Crispy Potatoes

Roast Chicken Leg with Tarragon, Cucumber and Cashew Salad

Ultimate Beef Burger

Pear, Blackberry and Walnut Crumble, with Pouring Cream

Caramelised Banana Split

Home Alone

Home Alone

This is one of my favourite chapters. When I was training I was always alone, and I was perfectly content getting on with my life. I was a focused young person, happy to be on my own, and that's probably what I prefer deep down inside. The dishes here are really personal, and they reflect how I like to cook for myself – because I'm a chef, I like to make lovely food to eat while I'm watching a movie or a sporting event. These recipes are fun, friendly and comforting at the same time. It's about enjoying precious quiet time alone.

Croque Monsieur

SERVES: 1 | PREP TIME: UNDER 10 MINUTES | COOKING TIME: ABOUT 20 MINUTES

My wife, Jane and I used to eat these a lot when I worked in France. They're always pre-prepped in cafes in Paris (and probably about ten days old!). A well-made Croque Monsieur is warm, it's toasty, it's crunchy, it's oozing with fat. It's the ultimate French toastie – and this one's a knockout. It makes a great supper, with a green salad on the side. I have used prosciutto instead of cooked ham in this recipe, as I prefer the flavour.

50g Gruyère cheese, grated
2 slices of sourdough
3–4 slices of prosciutto
10g butter

FOR THE BÉCHAMEL
100ml milk
1 tsp thyme leaves
10g butter
1 tbsp plain flour
½ tsp Dijon mustard
1 tsp wholegrain mustard
50g Cheddar cheese, grated
sea salt and freshly ground black pepper

1. Start by making the béchamel. Put the milk and thyme into a small saucepan. Gently bring to a simmer over low heat. Melt the butter in another small saucepan then add the flour, and a pinch each of salt and pepper. Cook over low heat for about 1 minute to get rid of the floury taste, but avoid letting it brown. Gradually whisk in half of the hot milk and stir quickly to combine. Add the remaining milk and cook for a further 5 minutes over low heat, stirring continuously. Remove from the heat, add the mustards and cheese and stir until the cheese has melted.

2. Preheat the oven to 200°C/180°C fan/gas 6.

3. Place the grated Gruyère on one slice of the sourdough then top with the prosciutto. Finish with the béchamel then top with the other slice of sourdough. Heat a frying pan over medium heat. When hot, add the butter then carefully add the sandwich and toast it for 3–5 minutes. Gently turn the sandwich over and brown the other side for another 3–5 minutes.

4. Transfer to a piece of baking parchment on a baking tray and bake in the oven for 4–5 minutes, until the cheese has melted.

Masterclass BÉCHAMEL SAUCE

If you've ever been to France and had a Croque Monsieur in a cafe, it was probably crap. But they can be delicious. You've just got to put in the effort to make the béchamel sauce. It takes some skill, and can become lumpy. Why? Well, it's simple – you've not cooked out your roux (butter and flour) properly, or you've added the milk too quickly. Once you've added the flour to the melted butter you really need to beat it well and work it really hard to bring them together to make that roux base. You're cooking the flour at the same time. Now it's like making a risotto – if you pour in all the milk at once, the roux could just split: the butter will separate from the flour and you'll have a disaster on your hands. You need to add a little bit at a time. It's also important to add hot milk to a hot roux, otherwise it will cool the roux right down. I use a wooden spoon in a heavy-bottomed pan over low heat.

Smoked Salmon and Garden Herb Omelette

SERVES: 1 | PREP TIME: 10 MINUTES | COOKING TIME: UNDER 10 MINUTES

Sometimes you want a little more than a plain omelette for supper – this recipe brings a few of my favourite things together. I would serve this with some spinach on the side, which has been sautéed in a little butter and nutmeg, and a nice glass of Chardonnay. See page 149 for my omelette masterclass.

10g butter
3 eggs, beaten
50g smoked salmon
1 small shallot, diced
½ tsp capers in brine, finely chopped
2 tbsp crème fraîche
finely grated zest of ½ lemon
2 tbsp finely chopped garden herbs (such as dill, parsley, tarragon and marjoram)
25g Cheddar cheese, grated
sea salt and freshly ground black pepper

1. Heat the butter in a medium non-stick frying pan over medium heat. When the butter has melted, season the beaten eggs with salt and pepper and pour them into the pan. Using a spatula, quickly move the egg around the pan until it begins to firm up. When the egg is almost cooked, lay the salmon over the top on one side then top with the remaining ingredients, as well as a good grind of black pepper. Leave to sit over the heat for 2 minutes.

2. Remove the pan from the heat and carefully fold the empty omelette half over the topped half. Allow to sit for 2 minutes then transfer to a warm plate and eat immediately.

Chop Chop Salad

SERVES: 1 | PREP TIME: ABOUT 5 MINUTES | COOKING TIME: ABOUT 5 MINUTES

We're not really a salad nation, we just open bags and tip them out. American chefs, however, really make great chopped salads. I first had a version of this salad at Daniel Boulud's restaurant in London and thought it was the perfect meal in a bowl. It had everything; freshness, crunch, sweetness, creaminess and such a great flavour. There is not really any cooking involved, apart from frying the croutons. It's a super-simple and fun meal for one.

20g cashew nuts
1 tbsp olive oil
1 small slice of sourdough (about 30g), diced
½ small (or ¼ large) iceberg lettuce, diced
1 slice of watermelon, diced (150g diced weight)
80g cooked chicken breast, diced
sea salt and freshly ground black pepper

FOR THE DRESSING
2 tbsp salad cream
1 tbsp crème fraîche
1 tbsp finely chopped flat-leaf parsley
1 tbsp finely chopped dill

1. Heat a small frying pan and once hot, toast the cashews for a minute or two until golden brown. Tip out onto a plate to cool then roughly chop.

2. Heat the oil in the same pan over medium-high heat. When hot, add the diced bread and season well with salt and pepper. Toast the croutons for about 5 minutes, until golden brown, then transfer to a sheet of kitchen paper to soak up excess oil.

3. In a bowl, make a dressing by mixing together the salad cream, crème fraîche and herbs, and season it with salt and pepper.

4. Place the lettuce, watermelon, cashew nuts and chicken in a large bowl. Add the dressing and toss to coat. Transfer to a serving bowl and scatter the croutons on top.

Prawn, Tomato and Chilli Linguine

SERVES: 1 | PREP TIME: UNDER 10 MINUTES | COOKING TIME: ABOUT 25 MINUTES

This recipe takes me back to Italian summer holidays where the tomatoes are like sweets and the pasta so fresh it melts in your mouth. It can be hard to recreate this without such great ingredients but I find baby plum tomatoes are the best substitute. Good-quality dried pasta is fine, but if you can get fresh it is a little quicker to cook.

2 tbsp olive oil, plus extra for drizzling
2 shallots, thinly sliced
1 garlic clove, thinly sliced
pinch of dried chilli flakes
200g baby plum tomatoes, halved
1 tbsp vodka
110g fresh tagliatelle (or 80g dried)
120g raw king prawns, peeled and veins removed
1 red chilli, deseeded and thinly diced
8 basil leaves, thinly sliced
sea salt and freshly ground black pepper

1. Heat 1 tablespoon of the olive oil in a medium frying pan over medium heat. When hot, add the shallots, garlic and chilli flakes and season with salt. Cook for about 10 minutes, until soft, then add the tomatoes and a little more salt, and black pepper, and cook for 8–10 minutes. Add the vodka and cook for a further 2 minutes. Turn off the heat and leave to sit.

2. Bring a medium-large saucepan of well-salted water to the boil. Cook the pasta according to the packet instructions, until al dente.

3. When the pasta is nearly done, heat the remaining tablespoon of oil in a large frying pan over high heat. When it's starting to smoke, season the prawns with salt and pepper, add them to the hot pan and colour them briefly on each side. Add the tomato sauce to the pan with the prawns and mix well, then add the fresh chilli and basil leaves and stir through. Check the prawns to make sure they're cooked.

4. Drain the pasta, add it to the sauce and mix well. Serve immediately.

MARCUS' TIP:
I sometimes think of chilli as a seasoning, such as salt and pepper. A small amount of it can really enhance a dish and add an extra layer of flavour.

Chicken Schnitzel with Celeriac Remoulade and a Fried Egg

SERVES: 1 | PREP TIME: 20 MINUTES | COOKING TIME: UNDER 10 MINUTES

Crispy chicken, an oozy yolk and a crunchy, tangy celeriac remoulade. My kind of dinner! You can prep the chicken ahead of time – buy four or five breasts, flatten them, coat them and put them in the freezer to pull out when you're ready to pan fry.

1 skinless, boneless chicken breast
1 tbsp plain flour, seasoned with salt and pepper
2 eggs, 1 beaten
30g dried breadcrumbs (panko or homemade from old bread)
4 tbsp vegetable oil
sea salt and freshly ground black pepper

FOR THE CELERIAC REMOULADE
¼ small celeriac, peeled and finely sliced into matchsticks
finely grated zest and juice of ½ lemon
½ tsp wholegrain mustard
3 tbsp good-quality shop-bought mayonnaise
1 tbsp finely chopped flat-leaf parsley

1. Cover your chopping board with clingfilm and place the chicken breast on top. Cover with a layer of clingfilm then, using a rolling pin, flatten the chicken breast until it's about 1cm thick.

2. Put the flour, beaten egg and breadcrumbs in three separate shallow dishes. Coat the chicken in the seasoned flour, then coat it in the beaten egg and finish with a generous coating of breadcrumbs. Put it in the fridge for 10 minutes.

3. Place the celeriac in a bowl and season it with a little salt. Add the lemon zest and juice and leave to sit for 5 minutes, then add the mustard, mayonnaise, parsley and a pinch of black pepper and mix well.

4. Heat 3 tablespoons of the vegetable oil in a frying pan large enough to fit the schnitzel over medium heat. When the oil is hot, carefully place the schnitzel in the pan. Cook for 3–4 minutes on one side until golden, then carefully turn it over and cook on the other side for a further 3–4 minutes, until cooked through.

5. Heat the remaining tablespoon of oil in a non-stick frying pan over medium heat. When hot, crack the second egg into the centre and cook it to your liking.

6. Serve the schnitzel with the fried egg on top and the celeriac remoulade on the side.

MARCUS' TIP:
Keep one non-stick frying pan purely for cooking things such as eggs, pancakes and delicate fish. Clean it gently and store without any other pans on top, or with a protective layer in between. This will preserve the non-stick effect.

Butter-roasted Cauliflower with Capers and Parsley

SERVES: 1 | PREP TIME: 10 MINUTES | COOKING TIME: 45 MINUTES

I hated cauliflower as a child, but as I got older I realised that it has a beautiful flavour. And when it's roasted properly, it goes from being something quite plain to something very delicious. The trick is to get as much colour on it as possible as it then takes on a nutty, caramelised flavour. This is a great recipe for an easy supper on your own, as the oven does most of the work!

1 small cauliflower, or ½ a large
  cauliflower (with leaves on)
30g butter, melted
25g whole almonds
1 tsp capers in brine
1 gherkin, finely chopped
2 tbsp finely chopped flat-leaf parsley
finely grated zest and juice of ½ lemon
1 tbsp olive oil
1 tsp gherkin pickle liquor
2 tbsp crème fraîche
sea salt and freshly ground black pepper

1. Preheat the oven to 220°C/200°C fan/gas 7.

2. Slice the leaves off the cauliflower and finely shred them.

3. Cut the cauliflower in half, from top to bottom and through the core, and place cut-side down in a baking dish just large enough to fit the two pieces. Drizzle the melted butter over the cauliflower halves then season them well with salt and pepper. Place in the oven and roast for 40–45 minutes, turning them halfway through and basting them with the butter, until they take on a deep golden colour, and are soft when a knife is inserted.

4. While the cauliflower is cooking, place the almonds in a small ovenproof dish and toast in the oven for 6–8 minutes until golden. Remove from the oven and roughly chop.

5. Place the remaining ingredients in a bowl and mix together. Add the cauliflower leaves.

6. To serve, place the roasted cauliflower on a plate and spoon over any remaining butter in the baking dish. Scatter the toasted almonds on top and place the caper, parsley and cauliflower leaf salad on the side.

Barnsley Chop, Roasted Fennel and Black Olive Tapenade

SERVES: 1 | PREP TIME: 10 MINUTES | COOKING TIME: ABOUT 20 MINUTES

Fennel seems to be a rather divisive vegetable. When we have it on the menu at the restaurants we often get requests for a dish to be made without it, but I love the freshness it imparts. Roasting it brings out its natural sweetness, so if you don't like it raw, do try it cooked.

10g butter
½ fennel bulb, cut into quarters
¼ tsp fennel seeds, crushed
1 Barnsley chop (brined if you wish – use ½ quantity of the brine on page 242)
1 tbsp vegetable oil
sea salt and freshly ground black pepper

FOR THE TAPENADE
6 pitted Kalamata olives, chopped
2 tinned or cured anchovies in oil, finely chopped, or ½ tsp anchovy sauce
1 small shallot, finely diced
4 mint leaves, finely chopped
2 tbsp olive oil
1 tsp balsamic vinegar

1. Preheat the oven to 210°C/190°C fan/gas 7.

2. Put the butter, quartered fennel and fennel seeds in a small roasting dish. Season with salt and pepper and place in the oven for 12 minutes.

3. While the fennel is cooking, bring the Barnsley chop to room temperature (rinsing off the brine and patting dry with kitchen paper, if the chop was brined). Heat the vegetable oil in a small heavy-based frying pan over high heat. When hot, season the chop on both sides with salt and pepper and place in the pan. Fry for around 5 minutes each side, until well browned.

4. After the fennel has been in the oven for 12 minutes, remove the dish, turn the fennel pieces over, then place the chop on top. Bake in the oven for a further 6–8 minutes then remove and allow to rest for 5 minutes.

5. To make the tapenade, mix together the olives, anchovies, shallot, mint, olive oil and balsamic vinegar in a bowl with a good grind of black pepper.

6. Serve the fennel, the chop, and the cooking juices with the tapenade.

MARCUS' TIP:
A Barnsley chop, or saddle chop, has a centre bone with two pieces of loin on either side. On top is a good layer of fat, and I recommend cooking the chops with this on, as it will render in the oven and enhance the lamb flavour. You can remove it on eating if you wish.

Sirloin Steak with Brandy Sauce and Crispy Potatoes

SERVES: 1 | PREP TIME: 10 MINUTES | COOKING TIME: 25–35 MINUTES

Cooking for one can sometimes seem a little too much effort, but this recipe is very much worth it. Sirloin is one of my favourite cuts of steak as it has such depth of flavour. I generally only buy dry-aged steak that has been matured for at least 21 days (this ageing further enhances the flavour) and I don't tend to brine quick-cook steaks like this.

5 new potatoes
2 tbsp olive oil
¼ bunch of thyme
1 tbsp vegetable oil
1 × 200–250g sirloin steak
20g butter, cubed
1 garlic clove, bashed
sea salt and freshly ground black pepper

1. Steam the potatoes for 15–20 minutes, until soft when pierced with a knife. Leave to cool.

2. Now, open all your windows!

3. Heat the olive oil in a small frying pan over medium heat. Cut the steamed potatoes in half and when the oil is hot, place them in the pan, cut-side down. Season well with salt and pepper and add a few sprigs of thyme. Fry for 10–15 minutes, turning them occasionally, until crispy on all sides.

4. While the potatoes are frying, or after, place the vegetable oil in a small, heavy-based frying pan over high heat. When smoking, season the steak on both sides with salt and pepper and carefully place it in the pan. Give the pan a gentle shake to ensure there is oil under the steak. Fry for about 2 minutes, until nicely browned on one side, then carefully turn it over and brown for another 2 minutes. Flip the steak back to the original side and add the butter, cube by cube, the garlic and half of the remaining thyme to the pan. When the butter starts to foam, tilt the pan towards you and spoon it over the steak. After 1 minute of basting, turn the steak over and baste the other side for a further minute. Remove it from the pan at this point if you like it more on the rare to medium-rare side, or if you prefer it cooked further, turn the heat down a little and continue to baste for a further 3–4 minutes (the cooking time will depend on the thickness of the steak, and the doneness you prefer). When you remove the steak from the pan, keep it somewhere warm and cover with another plate or foil to keep it warm.

FOR THE BRANDY SAUCE

2 shallots, thinly sliced
1 small garlic clove, finely grated
2 tbsp brandy
50ml good-quality beef stock
1 tbsp crème fraîche

5. Strain the contents of the steak pan through a fine sieve, discarding the garlic and thyme. Clean the pan and place back over medium heat with the strained pan juices. When the pan juices are hot, add the shallots, grated garlic, remaining thyme and a generous grind of black pepper. Cook for about 4 minutes, until the shallots are soft, then add the brandy and cook for a further 3 minutes. Add the beef stock and simmer for 3 minutes, remove the pan from the heat and pick out the thyme stalks. Lastly, stir through the crème fraîche. Taste the sauce, adding more salt and pepper if needed.

6. Your steak will be well rested at this point, and the potatoes crispy. Place the steak on a hot plate with the potatoes and pour the sauce over your steak.

Masterclass COOKING STEAK

People get nervous about cooking a steak, but it is a very simple thing to do if you follow this method.

First, buy a good piece of meat. Then, make sure it's at room temperature before you cook it – if you want it served medium or medium-rare you're not going to get it hot in the middle if it's fridge cold: take it out of the fridge a good couple of hours before cooking (meat doesn't go off unless it's been out for days). Now, place a heavy-bottomed pan over a high heat. Season the meat just before it goes into the pan, only seasoning the side that hits the pan first – if you season it in advance the salt will draw the water out of the meat, which will then spit at you from the pan and make the meat taste a little acrid rather than caramelised, as well as cooling the pan down. Place the steak in the pan and leave it for a couple of minutes. Don't be afraid of the smoke – it's inevitable. Shake the pan a little bit, then season the other side just before you turn the steak over. Turn it and cook it for another couple of minutes – you don't necessarily need to add butter – I put in a little bit of butter at this stage as a personal preference. The cooking almost crystallises the salt, giving it a little bit of crunch – you're looking for that umami-type flavour, the beautiful, hot caramelisation of the sugar of the meat and salt coming together to create that dark crispiness. Then add a little more butter if you wish, to cool the pan down a little, or just turn the heat down instead and cook for a further 2–4 minutes for a 2cm thick steak or 4–6 minutes for a thicker steak.

Never eat a steak hot – remove from the pan and let it rest for a good 5–10 minutes, then when you slice it the blood and juices will stay in the steak and it will be perfect.

Roast Chicken Leg with Tarragon, Cucumber and Cashew Salad

SERVES: 1 | PREP TIME: 15 MINUTES | COOKING TIME: ABOUT 40 MINUTES

I am a big fan of roast chicken legs, especially the crispy skin, which for me is the best part. You can substitute with a chicken breast if you prefer something leaner, but I like the flavour of the leg or thigh. The tarragon works well with the chicken, too.

1 large or (2 small) chicken leg(s) (brined if you wish – use ½ quantity of the brine on page 242)
10g butter, softened
¼ bunch of tarragon, leaves chopped and stems set aside
20g unsalted cashew nuts
100ml good-quality chicken stock
¼ cucumber, halved lengthways then cut into 5mm-thick half circles
½ gherkin, finely chopped
1 tbsp olive oil
splash of cider vinegar
½ tsp wholegrain mustard
1 tbsp crème fraîche
sea salt and freshly ground black pepper

1. Preheat the oven to 200°C/180°C fan/gas 6. Bring the chicken leg to room temperature (rinsing off the brine and patting dry with kitchen paper, if chicken was brined).

2. Mix the butter, half of the tarragon leaves, and a pinch each of salt and pepper together in a small bowl. Rub this under the skin of the chicken leg(s) then place the chicken in a small roasting dish. Roast in the oven for 30–35 minutes, until golden and the juices run clear, basting once, halfway through the cooking time.

3. While the chicken is cooking, put the cashew nuts in a small baking tray and toast in the oven for 8–10 minutes until golden, shaking halfway through. Remove from the oven and leave to cool, then chop roughly.

4. Also while the chicken is cooking, pour the chicken stock into a saucepan, add the tarragon stems, bring to a simmer and cook for 5 minutes. Remove from the heat and cover, to allow the stock to infuse for 10 minutes, then strain it into a jug and pour back into the saucepan.

5. Mix the cucumber, gherkin, olive oil and vinegar together in a bowl and set aside.

6. Once the chicken is cooked, remove it from the roasting dish and keep warm. Pour the chicken and tarragon stock into the roasting dish. Scrape the bottom of the dish, to remove any caramelised cooking juices then pour everything back into the saucepan. Place back over the heat and bring to the boil. Whisk in the wholegrain mustard and simmer for 2 minutes. Remove from the heat and stir in the crème fraîche and the remaining chopped tarragon leaves.

7. Season the cucumber salad with salt and pepper, add the cashew nuts then serve with the cooked chicken and tarragon sauce.

Ultimate Beef Burger

SERVES: 1 | PREP TIME: 10 MINUTES | COOKING TIME: UNDER 10 MINUTES

There are now so many home-delivery takeaway options in London that it does make it simple to just order what you want, when you want. In doing so, however, you lose control over what goes into your food (although don't get me wrong, I am partial to a takeaway pizza every now and then!). This burger ticks all the boxes for me, and yes, it takes more time than ordering a takeout, but nutritionally you stay in control.

1 tsp vegetable oil
25g cheese, such as Monterey Jack,
    smoked Applewood or Gruyère, grated
1 burger bun, halved
1 gherkin, sliced
2 leaves of butter lettuce
sea salt and freshly ground black pepper

FOR THE BURGER PATTY
150g minced beef
1 large shallot, finely diced
½ garlic clove, finely grated
1 tbsp finely chopped flat-leaf parsley
1 tsp capers in brine, finely chopped
1 tbsp Worcestershire sauce
a few drops of Tabasco sauce
¼ tsp smoked paprika
1 tbsp tomato ketchup

FOR THE MUSTARD MAYONNAISE
2 tbsp good-quality mayonnaise
1 tsp Dijon mustard
½ tsp wholegrain mustard
½ tsp sriracha sauce

1. Preheat the grill in your oven to medium.

2. To make the burger patty, put all the ingredients in a medium bowl and, using your hands, mix until combined. Shape into a patty just larger than the size of your bun.

3. Heat the oil in a small frying pan over medium-high heat. When hot, add the patty and fry for around 2 minutes until well browned, then carefully flip it over and brown on the other side for a further 2 minutes. Turn off the heat and allow the patty to rest in the pan.

4. Mix the mayonnaise, mustards, sriracha and a good grind of black pepper together in a bowl.

5. Place the burger patty on a small piece of foil on a baking tray. Gather the edges up a little so any juice won't run out. Top with the grated cheese and place halfway down in your oven to slowly grill the cheese. When lightly golden, remove the foil package and place the bun halves, cut side down, on the tray and grill until lightly toasted.

6. To assemble, place the patty onto the bottom bun. Top with the gherkin slices and lettuce. Spread half the mayonnaise on the top bun then press it gently on top.

7. Serve the burger with home-baked chips, the remaining mayonnaise (for dipping the chips into) and/or coleslaw.

MARCUS' TIP:
When you put your groceries away, plan ahead. If you know you are going to be cooking for one, portion out your meat and/or fish when freezing so you only need to defrost the amount you require.

Pear, Blackberry and Walnut Crumble, with Pouring Cream

SERVES: 1 | PREP TIME: 10 MINUTES | COOKING TIME: ABOUT 30 MINUTES

It might seem a little decadent to make a pudding for one but when you crave something sweet to finish a meal, this is a great option, and who doesn't love crumble? We had a bumper crop of pears on our trees this year so this recipe was a no-brainer for me. You could swap pears for other orchard fruits if you prefer.

30g butter
2 tbsp soft dark brown sugar
1 pear, peeled, cored and quartered
1 tbsp brandy
6 blackberries
20g plain flour
20g walnuts, finely chopped
¼ tsp ground cinnamon
20g caster sugar
single or double cream, to serve

1. Preheat the oven to 200°C/180°C fan/gas 6.

2. Put 10g of the butter and the dark brown sugar in a small saucepan that's big enough to accommodate the pear quarters in a single layer, place over low heat and allow it to melt. Lay the pear quarters flat in the caramel and pour the brandy on top. Cook over low heat for about 10 minutes, until the pears are almost soft when pierced with a knife. Add the blackberries and cook for a further minute.

3. Transfer the fruit mix to a pie dish or ramekin.

4. Put the flour, walnuts, cinnamon and caster sugar in a bowl, add the remaining butter and rub with your fingers until a crumble is formed.

5. Top the fruit with the crumble and bake in the oven for 10–15 minutes, until the topping turns golden.

6. Serve warm, with cold cream poured over the top.

MARCUS' TIP:
I like using a variety of alcohols when cooking sweet dishes: alcohol helps intensify flavours and cut through sweetness, creating a more balanced dish.

Caramelised Banana Split

SERVES: 1 | PREP TIME: 5 MINUTES | COOKING TIME: UNDER 10 MINUTES

What beats a classic banana split? There is only one thing: caramelising the bananas in dark brown sugar and rum. So that is what I have done here. Use the ripest bananas you can find, as they have much more flavour and natural sweetness. Ultimately, you don't really need to follow a recipe to make a banana split – we all know what we like – but this is my version.

1 tbsp soft dark brown sugar

1 tbsp dark rum

1 ripe banana, peeled and quartered
(cut in half lengthways, then each half crossways)

1 tbsp Nutella

15ml milk, warmed

50ml double cream

2 scoops of vanilla ice cream

1 tbsp toasted hazelnuts, finely chopped
(see page 235 for method)

1. Put the sugar in a small frying pan, add 1 tablespoon of warm water and place over medium heat. When the sugar has dissolved, cook for 1 minute, then add the rum and swirl to combine. Bring to a simmer. Place the banana pieces, cut-side down, in the caramel and shake the pan gently. Cook for 2 minutes, then turn the heat off and leave the banana in the pan.

2. Put the Nutella in a bowl and whisk in the warmed milk.

3. Whisk the double cream in a bowl until soft peaks form.

4. Place the bananas and caramel from the pan in a bowl. Top with the ice cream, whipped cream and Nutella sauce and finish with the toasted hazelnuts.

Blueberry Pancakes with Lemon and Honey Strained Yoghurt

English Muffin Pain Perdu with Crispy Bacon, Avocado and Sriracha

Welsh Rarebit

Goats' Cheese, Kale, Blood Orange and Mustard Salad

Branston Pickle, Onion and Cheddar Omelette

Prawn, Cos, Parmesan and Tahini Salad

Chicken with Seared Lettuce, Soft-boiled Egg and Cornichon Mayonnaise

Pizzas
Chorizo, Rocket and Crème Fraîche Pizza
Hummus, Aubergine and Roasted Pepper Pizza
Ham and Egg Pizza

Roast Chicken Breasts with Fennel Salad and Romesco Sauce

Pea Pesto and Chicken Spaghetti

Smoked Mackerel, Egg and Caper Fish Pie

Beef and Garden Herb Meatballs with Roasted Tomato Sauce

Rhubarb, Ginger and Almond Crumble

Apple and Membrillo Tart

Crêpes with Dulce de Leche Cream and Hot Nutella Sauce

In the Fridge

In the Fridge

There are thousands of dishes you can make in the home kitchen when you think you have nothing to eat, and this chapter is all about giving you some ideas. I once worked at a place called The Point in the Adirondack Mountains, New York state, where we had deliveries flown in once a week. We were in the middle of nowhere and had to learn how to be incredibly creative and resourceful with what was in the fridge, freezer or dry store. We would cook almost anything, and no customer had the same dish twice. Ever. This chapter is a nod to that time.

Blueberry Pancakes with Lemon and Honey Strained Yoghurt

SERVES: 4 | PREP TIME: 15 MINUTES, PLUS STRAINING
COOKING TIME: ABOUT 25 MINUTES

Brunch is one of those special treats, enjoyed with family at home, on weekends and on holidays. I'd take an omelette any day but some of my family adore pancakes, so I thought it only right to include a recipe in this book – they're indulgent and just delicious. To get the yoghurt super thick, it needs to be hung overnight, so you do need to plan ahead, but the pancakes themselves are very quick to make.

225g Greek yoghurt
finely grated zest and juice of ¾ lemon
3 tbsp runny honey, plus extra for
    drizzling

FOR THE PANCAKES
190g plain flour
2½ tsp baking powder
2 medium eggs
1½ tbsp honey
225ml milk
25g butter
125g blueberries

1. Line a sieve or steaming dish with a J-cloth or clean muslin and place over a bowl. Spoon the yoghurt into the J-cloth and cover with clingfilm. Place in the fridge for at least 6 hours, or up to 12 hours.

2. Remove the J-cloth from the sieve and scrape the strained yoghurt into a mixing bowl. Add the lemon zest and juice and honey and whisk until smooth.

3. To make the pancake batter, put the flour and baking powder into a mixing bowl. Make a well in the mixture and add the eggs and honey. Whisk until combined, then slowly add the milk, whisking well, until you have a smooth batter.

4. Heat a large non-stick frying pan over medium heat. Rub the pan with a knob of butter and when melted, add a large spoonful of batter (or 2–3 if your frying pan is big enough to cook a few pancakes at the same time). Press a few of the blueberries into the batter. Wait until the top of the pancake begins to bubble, then turn it over and cook until both sides are golden brown and the pancake has risen to become about 1cm thick. They should take 3 minutes per side to cook.

5. Repeat until you've used all the batter. You should have 12 pancakes.

6. Serve the pancakes with the lemon and honey yoghurt dolloped on top, and an extra drizzle of honey.

MARCUS' TIP:
You can use the liquid from the strained yoghurt in smoothies, to feed a sourdough starter or for fermenting and pickling vegetables, such as cabbage or carrots. It has natural bacteria in it and adds a great flavour.

English Muffin Pain Perdu
with Crispy Bacon, Avocado and Sriracha

SERVES: 4 | PREP TIME: 10 MINUTES, PLUS SOAKING
COOKING TIME: ABOUT 20 MINUTES

Eggy bread, the childhood English version of pain perdu, was one of my firm favourites as a kid. It was a great way to use up stale bread and also provided a filling and tasty meal. English muffins tend to be associated with eggs Benedict, but I wanted to do something a little different here.

4 eggs
225ml milk
4 English muffins, split into 2
12 rashers of smoked streaky bacon
25g butter
2 ripe avocados
1 tbsp sriracha sauce
2 tbsp crème fraîche
¼ bunch of coriander, leaves picked, to serve
sea salt and freshly ground black pepper

1. Crack the eggs into a bowl and add the milk. Whisk together and season with salt and pepper. Pour into a shallow dish that snugly fits 4 muffin halves. Add the muffin halves and soak on each side for 5 minutes. Once soaked, remove and repeat with the remaining 4 halves.

2. Preheat your grill to medium-high. Lay the bacon on a grill tray and grill until golden and crispy on each side.

3. Melt half of the butter in a large frying pan over medium heat. When hot, add 4 of the muffin halves and fry for about 5 minutes on each side until browned. Remove from the pan and keep warm in the oven. Repeat with the remaining 4 muffin halves.

4. To serve, halve, stone and slice the avocados. Divide the avocado slices amongst the muffin halves. Place 2 muffin halves on each plate and top with 3 rashers of bacon.

5. Whisk the sriracha sauce with the crème fraîche in a bowl and loosen it with a splash of water. Drizzle it over the top of the bacon. Finish with the coriander leaves and serve.

Welsh Rarebit

SERVES: 4 | PREP TIME: 5 MINUTES | COOKING TIME: ABOUT 15 MINUTES

It is fair to say Welsh rarebit has been around for a while and has most definitely stood the test of time. This recipe uses green chilli, as I think it gives a great contrast to the richness of the toast. Serve it for a weekend lunch or a quick supper – it's the ultimate snack or even the ultimate meal. I love the earthiness of it, but also the crunchy bread. I'd have this with a beer.

200g extra mature Cheddar cheese, grated
80ml Guinness, or your favourite beer
1 tbsp plain flour
1 tsp English mustard
1 tsp Worcestershire sauce
1 egg
4 thick slices of sourdough bread
1 green chilli, thinly sliced

1. Put the cheese and beer in a medium saucepan and place over low heat. Stir for 5–7 minutes until the cheese has melted, then add the flour and mustard and cook for 5 minutes, stirring frequently. Add the Worcestershire sauce and egg, remove from the heat and beat until smooth.

2. Preheat your grill then toast the bread lightly on both sides, keeping a close eye on it to ensure it doesn't burn.

3. Divide the green chilli between the 4 slices of toast then spread the rarebit mix on top. Place the toasts on a baking tray and grill until nicely golden. This should only take a few minutes, so don't leave them unattended. Serve straight away.

MARCUS' TIP:
Sourdough bread works best. I like the sourness of it, it holds the heavy mixture on top, and is able to withstand the cooking process. It also holds the moisture and richness and oiliness of the cheese when it starts to get hot. A sour cheese is similarly good to help cut through the richness.

Goats' Cheese, Kale, Blood Orange
and Mustard Salad

SERVES: 4 | PREP TIME: 15 MINUTES | COOKING TIME: UNDER 5 MINUTES

Blood oranges have a relatively short season, and are generally in supply in the UK at the end of winter and beginning of spring. They have a more complex and richer flavour than regular oranges and the most beautiful deep red flesh, and the zest is very flavoursome, but if they are not in season you can use regular oranges or pink grapefruit instead.

400g kale, tough stalks removed (or use ready-chopped kale)
2 blood oranges
1 tsp fennel seeds
2 tbsp wholegrain mustard
1 tsp Dijon mustard
50ml olive oil
½ tsp orange blossom water
2 tbsp pickle juice from a jar of gherkins
1 red onion, thinly sliced
160g hard goats' cheese, diced
¼ bunch of dill, fronds sliced
sea salt and freshly ground black pepper

1. Cook the kale in a saucepan of salted boiling water for 30 seconds. Drain and rinse under cold running water until cool. Drain again and pat dry with kitchen paper then slice.

2. Grate the zest from the oranges and set aside in a bowl. Place a sieve or colander over a bowl. Slice the pith from the orange and discard it then segment the oranges into the sieve or colander, reserving any juice.

3. Put the fennel seeds in a small frying pan and place over medium heat. Toast until fragrant then lightly crush using a spice grinder or pestle and mortar. Tip the crushed seeds into the bowl with the orange zest and add both mustards, olive oil, orange blossom water and pickle juice. Add the juice from the segmented oranges, whisk together and add a generous amount of black pepper and salt.

4. Lay the kale on a large serving platter then top with the orange segments, sliced onion and goats' cheese. Drizzle over the dressing and finish with the dill.

Branston Pickle, Onion and Cheddar Omelette

SERVES: 4 | PREP TIME: UNDER 10 MINUTES | COOKING TIME: ABOUT 25 MINUTES

An omelette is the ultimate quick but tasty dinner – see below for my omelette masterclass. I always have eggs, pickle, cheese and onions to hand so it makes a great last-minute meal. To give it some balance, I have it with a green salad on the side.

50g butter, cubed
1 onion, sliced
2 tbsp Branston pickle
10 eggs, beaten
80g Cheddar cheese, grated
pinch of dried chilli flakes
4 tbsp roughly chopped flat-leaf parsley
  (optional)
sea salt and freshly ground black pepper

1. Put half of the butter in a medium non-stick frying pan over medium heat. When melted, add the onion and season with salt and pepper. Cook for 6–10 minutes until golden, then add the pickle and mix well. Remove from the pan and set aside, wiping the pan clean afterwards.

2. Place half the remaining butter in the clean frying pan and put it back on the heat. When the butter has melted, add half the eggs, seasoning them well. Using a spatula, quickly move the egg around the pan until it begins to firm up. When the egg is almost cooked, spoon half of the onion and pickle mix on top, along with half the cheese and half the chilli flakes. Add half the parsley (if using) then leave for 2–3 minutes.

3. Remove from the heat and carefully fold one half of the omelette over the other. Leave it to sit for 2 minutes then transfer to a warm plate and cover. Repeat the process with the remaining ingredients.

4. Cut both omelettes in half and serve immediately.

Masterclass THE PERFECT OMELETTE

The perfect omelette requires four key things: fresh eggs, butter, a non-stick pan and a spatula. Believe it or not, the non-stick pan and the spatula are as important as the ingredients themselves.

Whisk the eggs thoroughly in a bowl and don't add any salt yet. Get your pan on the hob over medium heat – no hotter than that. If the pan's too hot, you'll brown the omelette. Put a generous knob of butter into the pan – make sure that the base of the pan is covered and the butter is really bubbling, almost to the point where it starts to go brown. Season the eggs and pour them into the pan. Gently move the egg mixture around with the spatula, don't whip it. What we love about omelettes and scrambled eggs is their texture. If the eggs are too whipped, they'll almost look split and they'll never come together as an omelette. You need to just gently manoeuvre the egg around the pan. The moment to flip it over is when the mixture becomes one, but is still a little bit runny. If you don't fold the egg over in the pan at this stage, it will just cook through from underneath – and you don't want that – as it takes a while to cook through, and the egg on the bottom of the pan will be overcooked and the omelette will just crack when it comes to folding it over. Remove from the pan immediately after folding.

Prawn, Cos, Parmesan and Tahini Salad

**SERVES: 4 | PREP TIME: 10 MINUTES, PLUS MARINATING
COOKING TIME: UNDER 10 MINUTES**

If you have the opportunity to purchase prawns in their shells (with their heads on) then you almost get a 2-for-1 ingredient. The heads and shells are so full of flavour, and make wonderful stocks, soups and sauces. And if you don't have time to use them at that moment, they freeze very well. This salad makes a perfect summer weekend lunch dish.

300g peeled raw prawns
2 tbsp harissa paste
1 tbsp olive oil
2 tbsp tahini
50g salad cream
50g crème fraîche
2 tbsp milk
¼ bunch of dill, fronds finely chopped
1 head cos lettuce, leaves separated and
   halved lengthways
25g Parmesan cheese
sea salt and freshly ground black pepper

1. Put the prawns in a bowl and add the harissa and olive oil. Stir, cover and marinate in the fridge for at least 1 hour (up to 6 hours).

2. Mix the tahini, salad cream, crème fraîche, milk and dill together in a bowl and season well with salt and pepper.

3. Heat a large frying pan or griddle pan over high heat. When it's almost smoking, season the prawns with salt and add half to the pan. Brown for 1–2 minutes on each side, until cooked through. Transfer to a bowl and repeat the process with the remaining prawns.

4. To assemble, lay the cos leaves on a large platter. Top with the tahini dressing, then the prawns. Shave the Parmesan over the top, using a potato peeler, and finish with a good grind of black pepper.

Chicken with Seared Lettuce, Soft-boiled Egg and Cornichon Mayonnaise

SERVES: 4 | PREP TIME: 10 MINUTES | COOKING TIME: UNDER 10 MINUTES

There is something so delicious about the combination of cooked chicken, lettuce, egg and mayonnaise. Hence I thought I should include an actual recipe for it in this book. It's the perfect meal, served with either hot or cold chicken, in summer or in winter.

4 eggs
100g good-quality mayonnaise
1 tsp finely chopped dill
7 cornichons, finely chopped
1 small shallot, finely diced
pinch of celery salt
1 tbsp olive oil, plus extra for drizzling
2 baby gem lettuces, halved lengthways
800g–1kg cooked chicken (1 small roast chicken, cold or hot, or other leftover meat), divided into 4
freshly ground black pepper
sourdough, to serve

1. Bring a small pan of water to the boil. Gently drop the eggs in and set a timer for 6 minutes for runny yolks. Drain off the water and sit the eggs (still in the pan) under cold running water for 1 minute, then leave them in the cool water.

2. In a bowl, combine the mayonnaise, dill, cornichons, shallot and celery salt. Add a good grind of black pepper and mix until combined.

3. Heat the oil in a large frying pan over high heat. When hot, add the baby gem lettuces, cut side down. Brown well for 3–5 minutes then turn off the heat and leave them to sit in the pan.

4. Peel the shells off the eggs.

5. Place the lettuce and chicken on 4 plates. Add the eggs, cut in half, and a good dollop of the cornichon mayonnaise. Drizzle with olive oil and serve with some good sourdough.

MARCUS' TIP:
For boiled eggs, the best way to ensure the shells peel off easily is to start with cold eggs from the fridge, plunged straight into the boiling water. Fresh eggs peel more easily too.

PIZZAS

MAKES: 2 LARGE PIZZAS (SERVES 4)

Nothing beats a good homemade pizza. And it's a great way to use up any odds and ends in your fridge. I have suggested a few different versions here but you can use these as a guide and add what you wish. It's a fun thing for a family to do together – in the summer, at weekends, on holiday. Everyone may like different toppings, in which case you can make smaller pizzas, or top each half according to personal taste.

200g Not-So-Ordinary Pasta Sauce (page 102)

1 tbsp olive oil

½ recipe of Pizza Base (page 103), either defrosted or fresh

2 tbsp semolina, or plain flour

1. Put the pasta sauce in a small saucepan over low heat, bring to a very gentle simmer and cook for 10–12 minutes until thick. Set aside.

2. Preheat the oven to 220°C/200°C fan/gas 7 about 10 minutes before the pizzas are ready to go in, divide the oil between two baking trays and place in the oven to heat.

3. Divide the dough in 2 and shape each piece into a circle. Dust with semolina or flour and roll out on a baking tray to as thin as you like your crust. Spread over the tomato sauce.

Chorizo, Rocket and Créme Fraîche Pizza

PREP TIME: 15 MINUTES, PLUS PROVING
COOKING TIME: ABOUT 20 MINUTES

120g chorizo, sliced or diced

1 red onion, thinly sliced

1 tsp capers in brine, roughly chopped

30g rocket, roughly chopped

2 tbsp olive oil

20g Parmesan cheese

6 tbsp crème fraîche, whisked

finely grated zest of ½ lemon (see tip on page 184)

sea salt and freshly ground black pepper

1. Once you've spread the tomato sauce onto each of the bases, add the chorizo, onion and capers then leave to prove at room temperature for 15–20 minutes until puffed up. Carefully slide each base onto the preheated and oiled trays in the oven (or bake them on the baking trays they proved on if you can't slide them) and bake for about 17 minutes, until pale golden.

2. Remove from the oven and top the pizzas with the rocket and olive oil. Finely grate the Parmesan on top then finish with a good grind of black pepper. Place in the oven for a further 3 minutes then remove and dollop the crème fraîche on top. Finish with the lemon zest and a touch of salt.

Hummus, Aubergine and Roasted Pepper Pizza

PREP TIME: 15 MINUTES, PLUS PROVING | COOKING TIME: 1 HOUR

1 aubergine
120g hummus
100g roasted peppers, thinly sliced
2 tbsp olive oil
3 tbsp finely chopped flat-leaf parsley
4 tbsp Greek yoghurt
2 tbsp pomegranate molasses
sea salt and freshly ground black pepper

1. Place the aubergine in a baking dish. Pierce it all over with a knife then place in the hot oven for 40 minutes.

2. While the aubergine is cooking, spread the hummus on each of the bases, followed by the tomato sauce (see opposite). Place the peppers on top then leave to prove at room temperature for 15–20 minutes until puffed up.

3. Slice open the aubergine, drizzle with the olive oil and season well with salt and pepper. Transfer (skin included) to a blender or food processor and pulse until a chunky purée is formed. Dollop this onto the 2 pizza bases.

4. Carefully slide each base onto the preheated and oiled trays in the oven (or bake them on the baking trays they proved on if you can't slide them) and bake for about 20 minutes until golden. Remove from the oven and top the pizzas with the parsley, yoghurt and pomegranate molasses.

Ham and Egg Pizza

PREP TIME: 10 MINUTES, PLUS PROVING | COOKING TIME: 20 MINUTES

120g cooked ham, sliced or torn
2 spring onions, trimmed and sliced
100g your favourite pizza cheese
    (Cheddar, mozzarella, Monterey Jack),
    grated
4 eggs
2 tbsp HP sauce
½ tsp wholegrain mustard
2 tbsp good-quality mayonnaise
handful of basil, leaves torn
sea salt and freshly ground black pepper

1. Once you've spread the tomato sauce onto each of the bases, leave to prove at room temperature for 15–20 minutes until puffed up. Carefully slide each base onto the preheated and oiled trays in the oven (or bake them on the baking trays they proved on if you can't slide them) and bake for about 12 minutes. Remove from the oven and top with the ham, the spring onions and cheese, making 2 recesses in each pizza for the eggs. Gently crack an egg into each recess then season with salt and pepper. Carefully place back in the oven for 8 minutes until the eggs are just set.

2. Whisk the HP sauce, mustard and mayonnaise together in a bowl with 1 tablespoon of water. Drizzle this over the top of the pizzas and scatter over the torn basil leaves.

Roast Chicken Breasts with Fennel Salad and Romesco Sauce

SERVES: 4 | PREP TIME: 15 MINUTES | COOKING TIME: UNDER 20 MINUTES

Romesco sauce is one of my favourite sauces. It works well with almost everything, including meat, fish, pasta and cheese, and works as a dip, too. I recommend always having the ingredients to hand for it as it is super quick to make and keeps in the fridge for a good few days.

4 chicken breasts, skin on
olive oil, for drizzling
sea salt and freshly ground black pepper

FOR THE ROMESCO
100g jarred/tinned piquillo peppers
50g flaked almonds, toasted (see page 16 for method)
3 tbsp olive oil
½ tsp smoked sweet paprika
2 tbsp chopped flat-leaf parsley
2 tsp tomato purée
splash of dry sherry, sherry vinegar or red wine vinegar

FOR THE FENNEL SALAD
½ tsp fennel seeds
2 tbsp olive oil
50g selected pickles (gherkins, onions, sauerkraut, cucumbers), finely chopped
2 tbsp pickle juice from a jar
1 large fennel bulb, trimmed and thinly sliced

1. Preheat the oven to 200°C/180°C fan/gas 6. Place the chicken breasts on a lightly oiled baking tray. Drizzle a little olive oil over the top of the chicken and season with salt and pepper. Cook in the oven for 14–16 minutes, until the juices run clear and the chicken is just cooked through. Leave the cooked chicken to rest for 5 minutes.

2. To make the romesco, put all the ingredients in a food processor or blender and blitz until you have a slightly chunky paste, or put them in a jug and blitz with a stick blender. Season to taste with salt and pepper.

3. Put the fennel seeds in a small frying pan over medium heat and toast until fragrant. Crush using a pestle and mortar and place in a bowl. Add the olive oil, pickles and pickle juice then toss the fennel through, seasoning well with salt.

4. To serve, cut the chicken breasts into thin slices and serve with the fennel salad and romesco.

MARCUS' TIP:
Toasted, or roasted, nuts are always significantly more flavoursome than untoasted. I suggest toasting or roasting them all when you get a fresh bag, then letting them cool and storing in an airtight container. It saves you needing to toast or roast them each time around.

Pea Pesto and Chicken Spaghetti

SERVES: 4 | PREP TIME: 10 MINUTES | COOKING TIME: ABOUT 15 MINUTES

This recipe deviates slightly from featuring things that are just in the fridge, using something I am sure you have in your freezer at all times – frozen peas. Frozen shortly after they are picked, peas are a very useful ingredient to have to hand as they are super versatile. I prefer frozen peas to fresh – fresh, raw peas work well in a salad, when they have a great crunch, but frozen peas have more flavour, and are much sweeter. Everyone associates pesto with basil, but I wanted to give an alternative. I use cooked chicken breasts here, as we always have some in the fridge.

360g fresh (or 400g dried) spaghetti
25g butter
2 cooked chicken breasts, shredded (about 250g)
100ml good-quality chicken or vegetable stock
sea salt and freshly ground black pepper

FOR THE PESTO

200g frozen peas
½ red onion, finely diced
1 garlic clove, finely grated
50g pine nuts, toasted (see page 34 for method)
½ bunch of basil leaves
25g Parmesan cheese, grated
50ml olive oil

1. To make the pesto, defrost the peas in a bowl of warm water for 2 minutes, then drain and put them and all the remaining pesto ingredients in a blender or food processor and pulse to form a chunky pesto. Season to taste with salt and pepper.

2. Bring a medium-large saucepan of salted water to the boil. Cook the pasta according to the packet instructions, until al dente. Drain and return to the pan.

3. While the pasta is cooking, heat the butter in a medium frying pan. When hot, add the chicken and the stock. Bring to a simmer and stir to combine the butter and stock. Simmer for 4–5 minutes until the chicken is hot.

4. Remove the chicken from the stock and add to the pan of pasta and mix well. Add the pesto and gently mix to combine. Serve while it's hot.

Smoked Mackerel, Egg and Caper Fish Pie

SERVES: 6 | PREP TIME: 30 MINUTES | COOKING TIME: 50 MINUTES

Mackerel is a great source of omega 3 and provides a quick protein fix when needed. A good fish pie is always a winner in my family so this ticks all the boxes. This recipe can be made a day or two ahead, then just heated through in the oven when needed. Depending on the time of year I would serve this with a simple green salad, or some steamed green vegetables.

4 eggs
300g baby new potatoes, scrubbed (or larger new potatoes, halved)
200ml good-quality vegetable stock
2 leeks, trimmed and thinly sliced
450–500g boneless smoked mackerel fillets, skin removed, flaked into chunks
2 tbsp capers in brine
bunch of flat-leaf parsley, leaves finely chopped
25g butter, softened
75g breadcrumbs (panko work well)
sea salt and freshly ground black pepper

FOR THE WHITE SAUCE
650ml milk
2 bay leaves
pinch of fennel seeds
½ nutmeg, finely grated
50g butter
50g plain flour
1 tsp Dijon mustard
2 tbsp wholegrain mustard

MARCUS' TIP:
White sauce, or béchamel, is a very handy thing to have on hand. Make a double recipe and keep it in the fridge for up to 3 days, or freeze. It's perfect for a quick supper such as pasta, a pie, making croquettes or lasagne. See my masterclass on page 118.

1. Bring a small pan of water to a rapid boil. Gently drop in the eggs and cook for 7 minutes. Drain and sit the eggs (still in the pan) under cold running water for 1 minute, then leave in the cool water.

2. Place the potatoes in a saucepan and top with water. Season well with salt and bring to the boil, then simmer for 18–20 minutes until cooked through. Drain and leave to cool.

3. Pour the vegetable stock into a saucepan and bring to the boil. Add the leeks and boil for 5 minutes, then drain, keeping the stock.

4. To make the white sauce, put the milk, reserved stock, bay leaves, fennel seeds and nutmeg in a medium saucepan. Gently bring to the boil over low heat. Remove from the heat and leave to infuse for a few minutes then strain into a heatproof jug.

5. Melt the butter in a saucepan and add the flour and a pinch each of salt and pepper. Cook over low heat, stirring, for about 1 minute to get rid of the floury taste, but avoid letting it brown. Add a ladle of the warm infused milk and stir to combine. Continue adding the milk a little at a time, stirring continuously, until you have a thick pouring sauce. Stir in the mustards and cook for a further 5 minutes over low heat, stirring constantly.

6. Place the mackerel, cooled potatoes and leeks in a large mixing bowl with the capers and parsley. Add the white sauce and gently mix until combined. Transfer to an approximately 26cm ovenproof pie dish or casserole dish.

7. Peel the shells from the eggs and quarter them. Press them into the top of the mackerel mix.

8. Mix the butter and breadcrumbs together and season well with salt and pepper. Top the pie with the crumbs in an even layer.

9. Preheat the oven to 200°C/180°C fan/gas 6.

10. Bake in the oven for 20–25 minutes until golden and bubbling.

Beef and Garden Herb Meatballs with Roasted Tomato Sauce

**SERVES: 4 | PREP TIME: 25 MINUTES, PLUS DRAINING
COOKING TIME: ABOUT 1 HOUR**

These flavoursome meatballs are not 100 per cent meat. Instead, they have a few other ingredients in them to bulk out the mix, and to add flavour and texture. With the intention to use up what's in the fridge and add nutritional value, the meatballs call for cooked grains or pulses. They are a great way to use up any leftovers and are perfect for vegetable-shy kids. Serve with spaghetti, jacket potatoes, rice or just a simple green salad. I would personally eat them with bread alone.

2 tbsp vegetable oil
100g full-fat cream cheese
4 tbsp milk
50g Cheddar cheese, grated

FOR THE TOMATO SAUCE

750g overripe tomatoes, halved
1½ onions, peeled and quartered
1½ tbsp olive oil
310ml tomato juice
sea salt and freshly ground black pepper

FOR THE MEATBALLS

2 courgettes, grated (400g)
1 tsp table salt
400g minced beef
100g cooked brown rice, barley, lentils or
 bulgur wheat
1 onion, finely diced
2 tbsp tomato purée
2 tbsp Worcestershire sauce
6 tbsp finely chopped herbs, such as basil,
 parsley, tarragon, dill, coriander
50g rolled oats
1 egg, beaten

1. Preheat the oven to 220°C/200°C fan/gas 7.

2. For the tomato sauce, place the tomatoes, quartered onions and olive oil in a large roasting dish, season with salt and pepper and roast in the oven for 15 minutes. Stir well, then roast for another 15 minutes. Transfer to a blender, add the tomato juice and blend until smooth. Adjust seasoning if necessary.

3. While the tomatoes are roasting, toss the grated courgettes in a colander with the table salt and leave to sit over another bowl for 10 minutes to drain. Squeeze as much moisture out as possible and place the courgettes in a large mixing bowl. Add all of the other meatball ingredients and mix well, using your hands (gloved if you wish). Divide the mixture into 16 equal portions and roll into balls.

4. Heat half of the vegetable oil in a large frying pan over medium-high heat. When hot, add 8 of the meatballs. Brown them all over for 5–7 minutes, then transfer to a 20 × 30cm baking dish. Repeat with the remaining meatballs and oil.

5. Pour the sauce onto the meatballs and place in the oven to bake for 10 minutes, until the sauce is bubbling.

6. While the meatballs are in the oven, whisk the cream cheese in a bowl until smooth. Add the milk and a good grind of black pepper and mix well. Fold in the grated cheese.

7. Remove the meatballs from the oven and dollop the cream cheese mix on top. Return to the oven and cook for a further 10 minutes.

8. Remove from the oven and serve with accompaniments of your choice.

Rhubarb, Ginger and Almond Crumble

SERVES: 4 | PREP TIME: 15 MINUTES | COOKING TIME: ABOUT 30 MINUTES

This is one of my favourite ways to eat rhubarb. The sourness of the rhubarb is perfectly balanced with the sweet, crunchy crumble. The only question left to ask is whether to have cream, custard or ice cream with it.

500g rhubarb, sliced into 3cm-thick sticks

3cm piece of fresh ginger, peeled and finely grated

2 tbsp honey

80g caster sugar

25ml amaretto (optional)

FOR THE CRUMBLE

125g plain flour

75g soft dark brown sugar

½ tsp ground cinnamon

½ tsp ground ginger

75g blanched almonds, toasted and roughly chopped (see page 126 for method)

75g cold butter, cubed

1. Preheat the oven to 200°C/180°C fan/gas 6.

2. Put the rhubarb, ginger, honey and sugar in a large saucepan over low-medium heat. Bring to a simmer, then cook gently for 10 minutes – there should still be some firmness to the rhubarb. Place in an approximately 24cm pie dish.

3. For the crumble topping, put all the dry ingredients in a mixing bowl. Using your fingers, rub the diced butter into the dry ingredients until the mixture resembles breadcrumbs.

4. Cover the rhubarb with the crumble and bake in the oven for 20–25 minutes until golden. Pour the amaretto over the top (if using) and serve.

Apple and Membrillo Tart

SERVES: 4 | PREP TIME: 15 MINUTES, PLUS CHILLING
COOKING TIME: ABOUT 20 MINUTES

As quinces contain such a high level of pectin, when cooked they naturally set. The resulting quince paste, membrillo, is generally served with cheese but it works well in puddings, too, such as this easy tart.

1 pack ready-rolled all-butter puff pastry
3 Braeburn or Pink Lady apples, peeled and cored
50g membrillo (quince paste)
25ml brandy
20g butter, cubed
vanilla ice cream, to serve

1. Roll the puff pastry out on a sheet of baking parchment into a rectangle about 3mm thick. Refrigerate for at least 20 minutes.

2. Preheat the oven to 200°C/180°C fan/gas 6.

3. Cut the apples into 2mm-thick slices, ideally using a mandoline.

4. Put the membrillo in a small saucepan with 4 tablespoons of water. Bring to a simmer and whisk the paste to form a thick purée. Add the brandy and butter and whisk until the butter has melted.

5. Remove the pastry from the fridge and place on a baking tray (still on the baking parchment). Leaving a 1cm border around the edge of the pastry sheet, prick it all over with a fork. Bake for 10 minutes until lightly golden. Place the apple slices, overlapping each other, on top of the pastry in 3 rows. Brush liberally with the membrillo paste and bake in the oven for 10–15 minutes until the apples are cooked and golden brown.

6. Remove from the oven and serve warm with vanilla ice cream.

Crêpes with Dulce de Leche Cream and Hot Nutella Sauce

SERVES: 4 | PREP TIME: 20 MINUTES | COOKING TIME: ABOUT 15 MINUTES

This is the ultimate treat. Warm crêpes with cool cream and hot chocolate sauce. It is a very simple recipe though, as most of the ingredients are already in your fridge or pantry, and there is not a huge amount of cooking involved, apart from making and cooking the crêpes.

FOR THE CRÊPES
130g plain flour
2 eggs
300ml milk
1 tbsp vegetable oil

FOR THE DULCE DE LECHE CREAM
4 tbsp dulce de leche
150ml double cream

FOR THE HOT NUTELLA SAUCE
4 tbsp Nutella
2 tsp cocoa powder
6 tbsp milk
4 tbsp chopped toasted hazelnuts (see page 235 for method)

1. To make the crêpe batter, place the flour and eggs in a mixing bowl and whisk together. Gradually whisk in the milk then transfer the batter to a jug. Allow the mix to rest.

2. To make the cream, put the dulce de leche in a medium bowl and whisk in 2 tablespoons of the double cream. Whisk the remaining double cream in a separate bowl until soft peaks form, then add it to the bowl of dulce de leche and fold it through to combine. Cover and refrigerate.

3. To make the hot Nutella sauce, put the Nutella, cocoa powder and milk in a saucepan. Place over low heat and bring to a gentle simmer, whisking. Simmer for 5 minutes, stirring often, until thick. Keep warm.

4. To cook the crêpes, brush a large non-stick frying pan with vegetable oil using a pastry brush. Place over medium heat and when hot, add a little of the mix from the jug and swirl the pan to distribute it evenly and create a thin crêpe. When lightly browned, and the top is no longer sticky to touch, gently fold the crêpe in half, then in half again and remove from the pan to a warm plate. Repeat until the mix is all used – you should have 8 thin crêpes.

5. Bring the Nutella sauce back to simmer then add the hazelnuts and remove from the heat.

6. Serve the 2 warm crêpes per portion with a good dollop of the dulce de leche cream and the hot Nutella sauce.

MARCUS' TIP:
We always have a jar of dulche de leche in our fridge (not just for the kids!). It is simple to make yourself, too, just boil an entire, closed tin of sweetened condensed milk for around 3 hours in a pan of water.

Lemon Curd Madeleines

Chocolate and Clementine Crunch Cookies

Hazelnut and Chocolate Choux Rings

Carrot and Parsnip Cakes with Orange Cream Cheese Frosting

Caramelised White Chocolate Brownie

Chocolate and Peanut Caramel Tray Bake

Date, Cardamom and Caramel Slice

Tahini and Caramelised Honey Cake

Blackberry and Buttermilk Cake

Blood Orange Meringue Pie

Rhubarb and Pistachio Frangipane Tart

Garden Focaccia

Green Olive and Fennel Seed Bread

Pumpkin Seed, Cumin and Cheddar Buns

Home Baking

Home Baking

These are the recipes I really enjoy making with my daughter, Jessie. She has always loved baking and she has a real knack for it. Jane's mum bakes, my mum bakes, Jane bakes, and now Jessie bakes – it has all followed through. She makes cakes for her brothers' birthdays, and when Jane and I had gluten- and egg-free diets she made gluten- and egg-free cakes for us. I particularly love the cookies in this chapter as they're one of the first things I made with my children. There are some lovely recipes here that all kids can get involved in – they're not too complicated and are fun to make together.

Lemon Curd Madeleines

MAKES: 12 LARGE MADELEINES | PREP TIME: 20 MINUTES, PLUS RESTING
COOKING TIME: 20 MINUTES, PLUS COOLING

Freshly baked madeleines are a delicious treat that is very hard to beat. Topping them with lemon curd makes them even more irresistible. I remember we used to have them on the bon-bon trolley at my restaurant, so giving them the taste-test was always important, especially just as they came out of the oven and were still warm. Any leftover curd will keep well in the fridge for a few days.

icing sugar, to dust

FOR THE MADELEINES
2 eggs
100g caster sugar
grated zest of 1 lemon
100g plain flour, plus extra for dusting
¾ tsp baking powder
100g butter, melted, plus extra for
   greasing

FOR THE LEMON CURD
80ml fresh lemon juice
50g caster sugar
1 egg, plus 2 egg yolks
80g soft butter, cubed

1. To make the lemon curd, put the lemon juice, caster sugar, egg and egg yolks in a medium heatproof bowl and set the bowl over a saucepan of gently simmering water, making sure the water doesn't touch the bottom of the bowl. Whisk constantly with an electric whisk until the mix is light and fluffy and begins to thicken to the consistency of custard. This will take about 10 minutes.

2. Remove the saucepan from the heat, with the bowl of curd on top, and whisk in the butter, cube by cube, until it is all incorporated. Pass the curd through a fine sieve into a clean bowl, cover the surface of the curd with clingfilm (to prevent a skin forming) and chill.

3. Using a pastry brush, grease a 12-hole madeleine tin with melted butter. Shake a little flour on top, to coat, tapping out the excess.

4. In a medium mixing bowl, whisk the eggs and sugar together with an electric whisk for 3–5 minutes until fluffy. Add the lemon zest.

5. In a separate bowl, mix the flour and baking powder together, then fold this into the egg mix. Add the melted butter and mix gently until a smooth batter is formed.

6. Cover the madeleine batter with clingfilm and place in the fridge for 20 minutes, to rest. Preheat the oven to 200°C/180°C fan/gas 6.

7. Divide the mix evenly among the moulds in the tin, and bake for 8–10 minutes until lightly golden and firm to the touch.

8. Release the madeleines from the tin as soon as you remove it from the oven, so they do not stick, and cool on a wire rack. Dust with icing sugar and serve with the lemon curd the same day they're made.

Chocolate and Clementine Crunch Cookies

MAKES: 18 COOKIES | PREP TIME: 15 MINUTES
COOKING TIME: 15 MINUTES, PLUS COOLING

Chocolate and orange is a classic combination that just works so well. Our kids get a chocolate orange in their stocking every Christmas – I'm sure Jane will carry on the tradition until they're adults. These cookies are crunchy on the outside and soft and gooey on the inside. If clementines are not in season, you can substitute them with one orange.

125g soft butter
100g granulated sugar
70g soft dark brown sugar
1 egg
grated zest and juice of 2 clementines or
   1 orange, plus an extra clementine
   (or small orange) for zesting
180g plain flour
25g cocoa powder
1 tsp bicarbonate of soda
100g dark chocolate (70% cocoa solids),
   cut into small chunks
4–6 tbsp icing sugar

1. Preheat the oven to 200°C/180°C fan/gas 6 and line 2 baking sheets with baking parchment or silicone mats.

2. Beat the butter and the sugars together in a bowl, using an electric whisk or a stand mixer, until light and creamy. Beat in the egg and clementine zest and juice. Sift in the flour, cocoa powder and bicarbonate of soda, stir to combine, then mix in the chocolate chunks.

3. Roll the dough into 18 golf-ball-size pieces then dip them into the icing sugar. Using the palm of your hand, flatten the balls onto the lined baking sheets, leaving space around each cookie to allow for spreading. Grate the zest of the extra clementine over the top of the cookies.

4. Bake in the oven for 12–15 minutes, until risen and nearly firm to the touch (they will firm up more upon cooling). Remove from the oven and leave to cool slightly on the sheets for 5 minutes before transferring to a wire rack to cool completely. Store in an airtight container for up to 2–3 days, or freeze.

Hazelnut and Chocolate Choux Rings

**MAKES: 8 CHOUX RINGS | PREP TIME: 30 MINUTES, PLUS COOLING
COOKING TIME: ABOUT 35 MINUTES**

A Paris-Brest is a choux ring piped full of the most delectable hazelnut praline cream. When I was living in Paris I used to gaze longingly at the patisserie counters and their endless window displays, filled with beautiful pastries as far as the eye could see. While most French pastries take a lot of work and skill, I found the Paris-Brest to be the easiest to recreate so developed this version to make at home.

icing sugar, for dusting

**FOR THE HAZELNUT AND
CHOCOLATE CREAM**
100g hazelnuts (skin off)
100g caster sugar
pinch of fine sea salt
4 tbsp Nutella
250ml double cream

FOR THE CHOUX BUNS
150g butter, plus extra for greasing
25g caster sugar
½ tsp fine sea salt
250g plain flour
4 eggs

1. Preheat the oven to 180°C/160°C fan/gas 4. Line a baking sheet with a silicone mat or baking parchment. Grease another baking sheet and set both baking sheets aside.

2. Put the hazelnuts in a roasting dish and bake for 10–12 minutes until they have taken on a deep golden colour. Remove from the oven, leave to cool, then roughly chop.

3. Put the caster sugar in a small heavy-based saucepan or frying pan. Place over medium heat and leave the sugar to melt and caramelise to a deep golden colour, swirling the pan occasionally to get even caramelisation (do not stir). Add the nuts and stir quickly to coat then tip onto the greased baking sheet to cool slightly.

4. Transfer the caramelised hazelnuts to a blender or food processor and blitz to form a smooth paste. Add a pinch of fine sea salt and the Nutella, blitz briefly, then transfer the paste to a bowl, cover and put the mixture in the fridge.

5. To make the choux buns, put the butter, sugar and salt in a medium saucepan with 250ml water. Bring to the boil to melt the butter, then turn the heat down to low and add the flour to the water mix. Using a wooden spoon, stir well and keep mixing until the mixture starts to leave the sides of the saucepan.

6. Remove from the heat and beat in the eggs, one by one. Transfer the mix to a piping bag fitted with a star nozzle and pipe 8 rings, each made of 2 piped layers of choux mixture and around 8cm in diameter, onto the silicone mat or parchment-lined sheet. Bake in the oven for 30 minutes until lightly golden and puffed and there is no give when you pick up the buns. Remove from the oven, turn off the oven and leave the choux to cool for 5 minutes. Then slice them in half through the middle and put them cut side up back into the cooling oven to dry out for 5 minutes (you might have to do this in batches). Transfer to a wire rack to cool.

7. Remove the hazelnut and chocolate mix from the fridge and beat in 50ml of the double cream. Whisk the remaining 200ml of cream in a separate bowl until stiff peaks form, then fold it into the hazelnut and chocolate mix. Chill in the fridge until the choux buns are completely cool.

8. Transfer the hazelnut cream to a piping bag fitted with a plain round or star nozzle and pipe onto the bases of the choux buns. Top with the choux lids then dust with icing sugar and serve.

Carrot and Parsnip Cakes
with Orange Cream Cheese Frosting

MAKES: 12 CAKES | PREP TIME: 25 MINUTES
COOKING TIME: 35 MINUTES, PLUS COOLING

This recipe is a great way to use up any old, and slightly soft, parsnips or carrots you may have lurking at the bottom of your fridge. As well as the more traditional carrot, parsnips add a floral sweetness so lend themselves well to a cake.

65g pitted dried dates
3 eggs
135ml vegetable oil, plus extra for
   greasing
195g plain flour
¾ tsp bicarbonate of soda
1½ tsp baking powder
2 tsp ground cinnamon
generous grating of nutmeg
135g caster sugar
135g carrots, peeled and finely grated
135g parsnips, peeled and finely grated

FOR THE FROSTING
100g soft butter
100g icing sugar
2 x 280g packs of cream cheese
grated zest of 2 oranges

1. Preheat the oven to 200°C/180°C fan/gas 6 and lightly grease a 12-hole muffin tin or 12 small friand moulds.

2. Put the dates in a small saucepan, cover with water and place over medium heat. Bring to a simmer and cook for 10 minutes until the dates are soft. Drain and blitz the dates in a blender or food processor to form a purée.

3. In a bowl, beat together the eggs, vegetable oil and date purée. Combine the flour, raising agents, cinnamon, nutmeg and sugar in a bowl. Add the grated carrots and parsnips, then add the date purée and egg mixture and stir until well combined. Spoon into the muffin tin or friand moulds. Bake in the oven for 20–25 minutes, until risen and just firm to the touch. A skewer inserted into the centre of one of the cakes should come out clean (it may take a little longer, depending on the moistness of the carrots and parsnips).

4. Remove from the oven and allow to cool in the tin or moulds for 10 minutes before turning out onto a wire rack to cool completely.

5. To make the frosting, beat the butter and icing sugar together in a bowl until light and fluffy.

6. In a separate bowl, beat the cream cheese and orange zest until smooth. Gradually beat in the creamed butter and sugar mixture. Place the icing in a piping bag fitted with a plain round nozzle.

7. Pipe the frosting onto the cooled cakes.

MARCUS' TIP:
To make the most out of all citrus fruits, if you are only using the juice, grate the zest and freeze until required.
If you are only using the zest then you can also freeze the juice in ice cube trays and add it to smoothies.

Caramelised White Chocolate Brownie

SERVES: 8 AS A PUDDING, 12 AS A TREAT | PREP TIME: 10 MINUTES, PLUS COOLING
COOKING TIME: ABOUT 40 MINUTES

Caramelised white chocolate has a wonderful caramel-like scent and incredible flavour. It reminds me of Caramac bars from childhood. To make it, you just bake white chocolate in a hot oven, stirring it frequently so it colours evenly. I will warn you now, the taste is quite addictive. I like these brownies best when they are served warm, with vanilla ice cream or crème fraîche.

300g white chocolate, broken into pieces, or buttons
180g butter, melted, plus extra for greasing
225g soft light brown sugar
2 eggs
210g plain flour
pinch of fine sea salt

1. Preheat the oven to 200°C/180°C fan/gas 6. Grease a 20 x 30cm baking tin and line the base and sides with parchment paper.

2. Line a baking tray with a silicone mat or baking parchment, place the chocolate on top and put the tray in the oven for 6 minutes. Remove, and using a rubber spatula, stir the chocolate. Repeat this step twice more, until you have a dark golden chocolate. Remove from the oven and allow to cool.

3. Mix the melted butter, brown sugar and eggs together in a bowl and beat until smooth. Fold in the flour and salt. Break up the cooled white chocolate into a mixture of small and larger chunks and fold it through.

4. Spoon the brownie mix into the lined baking tin. Smooth the top then place in the oven and bake for 20–25 minutes until golden and a skewer inserted into the centre comes out clean.

5. Remove from the oven and allow to cool slightly in the baking tin, then slice into 8 or 12 pieces.

MARCUS' TIP:
Brownies always taste better after being frozen – they tend to get denser and gooier. If you portion them before freezing you can take out squares as and when you want them, then just pop them in the oven or microwave to warm through.

Chocolate and Peanut Caramel Tray Bake

MAKES: 24 PIECES | PREP TIME: 15 MINUTES, PLUS COOLING
COOKING TIME: ABOUT 30 MINUTES, PLUS COOLING

What is not to love about chocolate, peanuts and caramel? This tray bake is moreish, and so easy to make as well. Use a combination of mixed nuts, such as almonds, pistachios and hazelnuts, instead of just peanuts if you like. This is a good bake to keep in the fridge for when a sweet treat is needed with a good cup of tea.

FOR THE BASE
125g soft dark brown sugar
150g soft butter
1 egg
1 tsp baking powder
230g plain flour
20g cocoa powder
200g blanched peanuts

FOR THE TOPPING
397g tin sweetened condensed milk
4 tbsp golden syrup
30g butter
½ tsp fine sea salt
75g dark chocolate, melted

1. Preheat the oven to 200°C/180°C fan/gas 6. Grease a 20 × 30cm deep baking tin and line the base and sides with baking parchment.

2. To make the base, beat the sugar and butter together in a bowl until light and creamy, using an electric whisk or a stand mixer. Add the egg and mix well. Combine the baking powder with the flour and cocoa powder and stir them into the mix until just combined. Press the dough into the lined baking tin to make an even layer and chill in the fridge for 20 minutes. Once chilled, bake in the oven for 12 minutes.

3. While the base is cooking, place the peanuts in a roasting tray and roast for 12–15 minutes until a deep golden colour. Remove the base from the oven and place the roasted peanuts on top of the cooked base.

4. Meanwhile, put the condensed milk, golden syrup, butter and salt in a medium saucepan and place over medium heat. Stir continuously until the butter has melted. Spoon the mixture on top of the peanuts and return the baking tin to the oven for a further 15–20 minutes until the mix begins to caramelise around the edges.

5. Remove from the oven and allow to cool, then drizzle the melted chocolate over the top of the caramel. Remove the traybake from the tin, cut into 24 rectangles and store in the fridge.

Date, Cardamom and Caramel Slice

SERVES: 8–12 | PREP TIME: 35 MINUTES, PLUS COOLING
COOKING TIME: 55 MINUTES, PLUS COOLING

This is like an afternoon tea version of sticky date pudding, with an added hit of cardamom. It is a sweet treat that is best enjoyed with a cuppa. Try a little Greek yoghurt on the side, too – a welcome hit of cool acidity to balance the sweetness.

FOR THE PASTRY

85g soft butter, plus extra for greasing
115g caster sugar
225g plain flour, plus extra for dusting
1 tsp baking powder
½ tsp fine table salt
100ml double cream

FOR THE DATE CARAMEL

130g pitted dates
100g soft dark brown sugar
50g double cream
½ tsp fine table salt

FOR THE CARDAMOM FILLING

4 green cardamom pods
100g caster sugar
100g soft butter
2 eggs
pinch of sea salt
115g ground almonds

1. To make the pastry, mix the butter and sugar together in a bowl until just combined (with your hands or with a wooden spoon). Sift the flour, baking powder and table salt together then add half of the dry mixture to the butter and sugar and mix to form a smooth paste. Add the remaining dry mixture and mix until fine crumbs are formed. Gradually add the cream, mixing just enough to bind to a dough. Shape the dough into a rectangle, wrap it in clingfilm and chill for 30 minutes.

2. While the pastry is in the fridge, make the date caramel. Put 100g of the dates in a small saucepan, cover with water and place over medium heat. Bring to a simmer and cook for 10 minutes until the dates are soft. Drain and blitz the dates in a blender or food processor to form a purée.

3. Put the soft dark brown sugar in a small heavy-based saucepan or frying pan. Place over medium heat and leave the sugar to melt and caramelise to a deep golden colour, swirling the pan occasionally to get even caramelisation (do not stir). Add the cream and table salt and whisk well to combine. Add the date purée and mix to form a sticky sauce, then remove from the heat.

4. Grease a 20 × 30cm baking tin and line the base and sides with baking parchment. Roll out the chilled pastry on a flour-dusted surface to fit in the base of the baking tin. Take the pastry rectangle and gently place it in the baking tin, prick all over with the prongs of a fork and chill for a further 30 minutes.

5. Preheat the oven to 200°C/180°C fan/gas 6. Bake the pastry for 15 minutes, remove from the oven and cool for 30 minutes.

6. While the pastry is baking, prepare the cardamom filling. Crush the cardamom pods using a pestle and mortar or a spice grinder, removing the pods and grinding the seeds to a fine powder. Beat the seeds with the sugar and butter in a bowl, by hand or in the bowl of a stand mixer, until light and creamy, then add the eggs, one at a time, beating well after each addition. Finally, add the sea salt and ground almonds and mix well. Cover the bowl with clingfilm and place in the fridge for 20 minutes.

7. Spread the date caramel onto the cooked, cooled pastry base then cover with the cardamom filling, smoothing out the top. Finely chop the remaining 30g of dates and place these evenly on top of the filling.

8. Bake in the oven for 30 minutes, until deep golden and the cardamom mix has just set in the centre. Remove from the oven and leave to cool in the tin before slicing.

Tahini and Caramelised Honey Cake

SERVES: 8–10 | PREP TIME: 15 MINUTES
COOKING TIME: 30 MINUTES, PLUS COOLING

Tahini is made by grinding sesame seeds to form a paste. It has a lovely, nutty taste and creamy texture, lending itself well for use in both sweet and savoury dishes. It adds an interesting twist to this recipe and enhances the other flavours throughout the cake. Burning honey or caramelising it emphasises its floral flavour and reduces its sweetness, making for a richer result. The black sesame seeds in the crumb are a beautiful addition to the cake but if you only have white sesame seeds these also work well.

FOR THE SESAME CRUMB

40g plain flour
40g black sesame seeds, toasted (see page 190 for method)
30g demerara sugar
1 tsp ground cinnamon
pinch of fine sea salt
40g butter, melted, plus extra for greasing

FOR THE CAKE

220g honey
120ml milk
100g tahini
2 eggs, beaten
200g plain flour
1 tbsp baking powder

1. Preheat the oven to 200°C/180°C fan/gas 6 and grease a 20cm round cake tin with butter.

2. Place the sesame seeds in a roasting tray and toast in theoven for 6–8 minutes until they start to colour.

3. To make the sesame crumb, mix all of the dry ingredients together in a bowl. Add the melted butter to mix together. Set aside.

4. For the cake, place the honey in a medium saucepan over medium-high heat. Bring to a rapid simmer and let it continue simmering for 4–5 minutes until it starts to darken to a deep golden colour. Remove from the heat and take out 4 tablespoons, setting this aside. Add the milk to the honey left in the pan, mix well, then mix in the tahini and eggs.

5. Mix the flour and baking powder together then fold in the honey mixture and mix until just combined.

6. Place half of the sesame crumb into the cake tin, crumbling it in as opposed to spreading it. Place half of the cake mix on top of the crumb. Repeat with the remaining crumb and cake mix.

7. Bake in the oven for 20–25 minutes, until a skewer inserted into the middle of the cake comes out clean.

8. Remove from the oven and leave to cool in the tin for 15 minutes, then turn the cake out onto a wire rack.

9. Reheat the 4 tablespoons of honey you reserved earlier and drizzle it over the slightly warm cake. Enjoy warm.

MARCUS' TIP:
Try substituting the sesame seeds and tahini with finely chopped toasted peanuts and smooth peanut butter. Just loosen the peanut butter down with a little water before adding it to the honey and milk, so the consistency is similar to tahini.

Blackberry and Buttermilk Cake

SERVES: 10–12 | PREP TIME: 25 MINUTES
COOKING TIME: 1 HOUR 10 MINUTES, PLUS COOLING

Buttermilk, traditionally, is the leftover liquid from the butter-churning process. As our butter is cultured in the UK, the buttermilk has a lovely tangy flavour while providing a little richness. If you are unable to source it, combining low-fat, natural yoghurt with an equal quantity of milk will give you a product similar in flavour and consistency.

200g soft butter, plus extra for greasing
390g demerara sugar
350g plain flour
1 tsp baking powder
½ tsp bicarbonate of soda
4 eggs
200ml buttermilk
grated zest and juice of 2 lemons
3½ tbsp blackberry jam
250g blackberries

FOR THE ICING
25g soft unsalted butter
25g icing sugar
150g cream cheese

1. Preheat the oven to 200°C/180°C fan/gas 6 and grease and line a 23cm springform cake tin.

2. Beat the butter and demerara sugar together in a bowl with an electric whisk, or in the bowl of a stand mixer fitted with the whisk attachment, for 5–7 minutes, until light and fluffy. Combine the flour, baking powder and bicarbonate of soda in a bowl.

3. Gradually add the eggs to the butter and sugar, beating well after each addition. Add a third of the buttermilk, and lemon zest and juice, and stir well, then add a third of the flour mixture, mixing well but taking care not to over-mix. Continue adding the remaining buttermilk and flour mixture, a little at a time, until just combined.

4. Spread the blackberry jam on the bottom of the greased cake tin. Place the blackberries in the jam, bottom side down and evenly spaced. Spoon over the cake mix and smooth over until flat. Bake in the oven for 1 hour–1 hour 10 minutes, until the cake is just firm in the centre and a skewer inserted into the middle of the cake comes out clean. Cover the cake loosely with foil after about 40 minutes to prevent it from going too dark. Remove from the oven and leave to cool in the tin for 15 minutes, then turn out onto a wire rack and leave to cool completely.

5. To make the icing, beat the butter and icing sugar together in a bowl with an electric whisk, or in the bowl of a stand mixer, until light and creamy. Add the cream cheese and mix until combined. Place the icing in a piping bag fitted with a plain round nozzle and pipe rounds of icing onto the cake.

Blood Orange Meringue Pie

**SERVES: 10 | PREP TIME: ABOUT 40 MINUTES, PLUS CHILLING
COOKING TIME: ABOUT 1¼ HOURS**

This is my favourite bake. My mum and my nan both used to make lemon meringue pie, and I just love the flavour of it, but using blood orange instead of lemon makes it richer and not as tart or tangy. Blood oranges are in season at the very beginning of spring. The new-season ones have a lesser red tone than when the season gets in full swing, but are just as delicious. If they are unavailable, you can use any orange in this recipe, but you will lose the pale pink hue the blood oranges give to the curd.

FOR THE PASTRY
250g plain flour, plus extra for dusting
pinch of fine sea salt
160g cold butter, cubed
75g caster sugar
1 egg, beaten, plus 1 egg yolk

FOR THE BLOOD ORANGE CURD
grated zest and juice of 4 blood oranges
　(275ml)
300ml orange juice
75g cornflour
4 egg yolks
80g caster sugar
50g soft butter, cubed
5 drops Angostura bitters

1. To make the pastry, rub together the flour, salt and cold butter in a bowl until the mixture has a breadcrumb-like texture (or blitz in a food processor). Stir in the sugar and gradually add the beaten egg to form a soft, pliable dough (you will not need all the egg). Wrap the dough in clingfilm and chill for 30 minutes.

2. Roll out the pastry on a lightly floured surface until 3–5mm thick and use it to line a 25cm loose-bottomed tart tin, leaving a little excess pastry to hang over the edges. Return to the fridge for 20 minutes.

3. Preheat the oven to 240°C/220°C fan/gas 8.

4. Line the chilled pastry case with baking parchment and fill with baking beans. Sit the tart case on a baking sheet and bake for 5 minutes. Reduce the oven temperature to 200°C/180°C fan/gas 6 and bake the tart case for a further 10–15 minutes, until it starts to turn golden and become firm. Remove the baking beans and parchment, brush with the egg yolk and return to the oven for a further 5 minutes, until evenly golden. Remove from the oven and allow to cool slightly. When cool enough to handle, trim away the excess pastry with a sharp knife.

5. To make the blood orange curd, put the orange zest and juices in a saucepan. Put the cornflour in a small bowl, along with 6 tablespoons of the orange juice mixture, and mix well until smooth. Add the cornflour mixture to the saucepan. Place over medium heat and stir continuously until the mixture begins to thicken. When thick, add the egg yolks and sugar and stir over low heat for a further 4 minutes. Remove from the heat and whisk in the butter, cube by cube. Add the Angostura bitters and remove from the heat. Pour the curd into the cooked tart shell.

FOR THE MERINGUE

1 lemon wedge
4 egg whites
200g caster sugar

6. Turn the oven down to 170°C/150°C fan/gas 4.

7. To make the meringue, rub the lemon wedge around the inside of a spotlessly clean mixing bowl or the bowl of a stand mixer. Add the egg whites and whisk on high speed until they form stiff peaks, then decrease the mixing speed to medium and gradually add the sugar, whisking continuously. Whisk for 10–15 minutes until you have a stiff meringue and all the grains of sugar have dissolved.

8. Dollop spoonfuls of the meringue mixture onto the curd, swirling to create peaks. Bake in the oven for 45 minutes–1 hour until the meringue is crispy on the outside. Remove from the oven and allow to cool before removing from the tin and slicing.

Rhubarb and Pistachio Frangipane Tart

SERVES: 10 | PREP TIME: 35 MINUTES, PLUS CHILLING
COOKING TIME: ABOUT 1 HOUR 25 MINUTES

The vibrant green and pink tones in this tart, from the pistachios and the rhubarb, make this a rather show-stopping creation. And it tastes delicious – the slight sourness of the rhubarb, combined with the sweet and nutty frangipane, makes it a dish you will want to go back to for second helpings!

FOR THE PASTRY
175g plain flour, plus extra for dusting
pinch of fine sea salt
115g cold butter, cubed
50g caster sugar
1 egg, beaten
1 egg yolk

FOR THE RHUBARB
200g caster sugar
2 tbsp grenadine
400g rhubarb, cut into 4cm pieces

FOR THE FRANGIPANE
100g caster sugar
100g soft butter
2 eggs
125g shelled pistachios
pinch of sea salt

MARCUS' TIP:
When working with pastry you need to be as quick as you can, and touch it as little as possible. Any heat, from your hands or the air, will soften it, thus making it difficult to roll and line a tart case with. If it starts to get too soft and tricky to work with, pop it back in the fridge for 10 minutes at a time to firm up again.

1. To make the pastry, rub together the flour, salt and cold butter in a bowl until the mixture has a breadcrumb-like texture (or blitz in a food processor). Stir in the sugar and gradually add the beaten egg to form a soft, pliable dough (you will not need all the egg). Wrap the dough in clingfilm and chill for 30 minutes.

2. Roll out the pastry on a lightly floured surface to a thickness of 3–5mm and use it to line a 23cm loose-bottomed tart tin, leaving a little excess pastry to hang over the edges. Return to the fridge for 20 minutes.

3. Preheat the oven to 240°C/220°C fan/gas 8.

4. Line the chilled pastry case with baking parchment and fill with baking beans. Sit the tart case on a baking sheet and bake for 5 minutes. Reduce the oven temperature to 200°C/180°C fan/gas 6 and bake the tart case for a further 10–15 minutes, until it starts to turn golden and become firm. Remove the baking beans and parchment, brush with the egg yolk and return to the oven for a further 5 minutes, until evenly golden. Remove from the oven and allow to cool slightly. When cool enough to handle, trim away the excess pastry with a sharp knife.

5. To cook the rhubarb, put the caster sugar and grenadine in a large saucepan. Top up with 400ml water and bring to a simmer over medium-high heat, stirring to dissolve the sugar. Place the rhubarb pieces in the hot liquid and simmer for 3 minutes, then remove the pan from the heat and allow the rhubarb to continue to cook in the liquid for 5 minutes. Carefully transfer the rhubarb from the liquid into a bowl using a slotted spoon and place in the fridge to cool. Place the saucepan of cooking liquor back on the heat and bring to a rapid boil. Boil until syrupy – keep a close eye on it towards the end to prevent it burning. Remove from the heat and set aside.

6. To make the frangipane, beat together the sugar and butter in a bowl until light and creamy. Add the eggs one at a time, beating well after each addition. Put the pistachios in a blender and pulse until they have a breadcrumb-like texture, then mix them into the butter mix with the salt.

7. Spread the frangipane on the bottom of the pastry case then gently press in the cooked rhubarb pieces. Bake in the oven for 45–50 minutes, until deep golden and the frangipane has just set in the centre. Remove from the oven and leave to cool to room temperature before removing the tart from the tin. Warm the reduced rhubarb cooking liquor and brush it over the tart before serving.

Garden Focaccia

**MAKES: 1 LARGE FOCACCIA | PREP TIME: 20 MINUTES, PLUS RISING AND PROVING
COOKING TIME: ABOUT 25 MINUTES**

Freshly baked, herb-infused bread smells so wonderful. It takes some willpower not to sit down with a bowl of good olive oil and eat your way through a generous portion of it as soon as it's out of the oven. It's Italian in style and very simple and straightforward to make. In this recipe, I encourage you to do a little mixing and matching. Herbs work well, of course, but also vegetables and fruit – a few of my favourite additions are cherry tomatoes, gooseberries, blackcurrants, fennel and asparagus. Practically your five a day.

300g strong bread flour, plus extra for dusting

1 tsp table salt

30ml olive oil, plus 30ml for drizzling

7g sachet fast-action dried yeast or 23g fresh yeast

1 tbsp finely chopped flat-leaf parsley

1 tbsp finely chopped rosemary

1 tbsp finely chopped dill

20cm piece of rhubarb, cut into 1cm-thick slices

1 red onion, thinly sliced

½ courgette, sliced lengthways into 3–5mm strips (around 4 strips)

1 tsp flaked sea salt, for the top of the bread

12–16 basil leaves

2 tbsp honey, for drizzling

1. Mix together the flour and table salt in a bowl.

2. In a jug, combine 150ml tepid water with the olive oil and yeast (crumbling in the fresh yeast, if using) and mix together. Make a well in the flour and pour the liquid into the well. Mix to form a soft dough that leaves the sides of the bowl. Knead for 7–10 minutes, until smooth. This can be done by hand on a lightly floured surface or using a stand mixer fitted with a dough hook.

3. Lightly grease the inside of a bowl with oil, place the dough in it and cover the bowl with lightly oiled clingfilm. Leave to rise in a warm place for about 1 hour, or until the dough has doubled in size.

4. Once the dough has risen, add the chopped herbs to the bowl and knead them through the dough.

5. Turn out the dough onto a floured work surface and roll it out into a large rectangle, approximately 18 × 30cm and 1cm thick. Push the rhubarb into the dough and top with the onion, courgette and two-thirds of the olive oil. Sprinkle with salt, place on a well-floured baking tray, cover loosely with oiled clingfilm and leave in a warm place to prove for 30 minutes.

6. While the dough is proving, preheat the oven to 240°C/220°C fan/gas 8 with a heavy baking tray inside. After 20 minutes, drizzle the remaining olive oil on the tray and place it back in the oven.

7. Carefully remove the hot, oiled tray from the oven and slide the proved dough onto it. Turn the oven down to 220°C/200°C fan/gas 7 and bake for 15 minutes. Remove from the oven, top with the basil leaves and drizzle with the honey and return to the oven for a further 10 minutes.

8. Remove from the oven and leave to cool slightly before serving.

Green Olive and Fennel Seed Bread

**MAKES: 1 LARGE LOAF | PREP TIME: ABOUT 20 MINUTES, PLUS RISING AND PROVING
COOKING TIME: 30 MINUTES**

This versatile bread is great for sandwiches, toast and also just to eat with some good olive oil. We have a fennel seed bread we have served at our restaurants for quite some time and it creates a very subtle aniseed flavour, without overpowering. If you are not a fennel fan, I would still encourage you to try it. But if you really must, you can swap it for some finely chopped rosemary or thyme.

1 tbsp fennel seeds

300g strong white flour, plus extra for dusting

200g wholemeal flour

7g sachet fast-action dried yeast or 23g fresh yeast

1 tbsp soft dark brown sugar

2 tsp table salt

50ml olive oil, plus extra for greasing and drizzling

100g green olives, sliced

1. Put the fennel seeds in a small frying pan over medium heat and toast for 3–4 minutes until fragrant, moving them gently. Tip them into a mortar and lightly crush with pestle, or grind in a spice grinder. Mix the fennel with the flours, yeast (crumbling the fresh yeast, if using), sugar and salt in a bowl, then add the olive oil and 275ml of tepid water and mix to form a soft, smooth dough that leaves the sides of the bowl. Knead for about 10 minutes, until dough is smooth. This can be done by hand on a lightly floured surface or using a stand mixer fitted with a dough hook.

2. Lightly grease the inside of a clean bowl with oil, place the dough in it and cover the bowl with lightly oiled clingfilm. Leave to rise in a warm place for 1–1½ hours, or until the dough has doubled in size.

3. Turn out the risen dough onto a floured surface, knock it back, add half the olives and knead it into a long oval-shaped loaf about 25cm long. Arrange the remaining sliced olives on top then transfer to a floured baking sheet. Drizzle the loaf with a little more olive oil, then cover it loosely with clingfilm and leave to prove in a warm place for about 30 minutes.

4. While the dough is proving, preheat the oven to 210°C/190°C fan/gas 7.

5. Once proved, bake the bread in the oven for 25–30 minutes until golden. Remove from the oven, transfer to a wire rack and leave to cool.

MARCUS' TIP:
Freshly baked, homemade bread is a great way to introduce kids to brown bread if you are finding they are reluctant to eat shop-bought brown bread. Leave out the olives if they don't like them. Serve it warm, with their favourite topping.

Pumpkin Seed, Cumin and Cheddar Buns

**MAKES: 12 BUNS | PREP TIME: 25 MINUTES, PLUS RISING
COOKING TIME: 30 MINUTES**

Pumpkin seeds are loaded with nutrients and are a great way to add texture to any dish. These buns are like pinwheels, and the colour of the seeds makes them rather eye-catching. If you like, you can freeze the whole roll, then defrost and slice for a quick bake – they make a great accompaniment to a bowl of delicious soup for a winter's lunch.

FOR THE DOUGH

1 tbsp cumin seeds, plus extra for dusting
500g strong white flour
7g sachet fast-action dried yeast or 23g
   fresh yeast
1 tbsp caster sugar
2 tsp fine sea salt, plus extra for seasoning
50ml olive oil, plus extra for greasing

FOR THE PUMPKIN SEED PASTE

120g pumpkin seeds
2 tbsp pumpkin seed oil
150g Cheddar cheese, grated
sea salt and freshly ground black pepper

1. Put the cumin seeds in a small frying pan over medium heat and toast for 3–4 minutes until fragrant, moving them gently. Tip them into a mortar and lightly crush with pestle, or grind in a spice grinder. Mix the cumin with the flour, yeast, sugar, salt, olive oil and 275ml of tepid water in a bowl to form a soft, smooth dough that leaves the sides of the bowl. Knead for about 10 minutes, until dough is smooth. This can be done by hand on a lightly floured surface or using a stand mixer fitted with a dough hook.

2. Lightly grease the inside of a bowl with oil, place the dough in it and cover the bowl with lightly oiled clingfilm. Leave to rise in a warm place for about 1 hour, or until it has doubled in size.

3. Towards the end of the rising time, preheat the oven to 200°C/180°C fan/gas 6. Place the pumpkin seeds in a roasting tray and toast in the oven for 10–12 minutes until they start to pop. Set aside 20g of the seeds and put the remaining 100g in a blender or food processor with the pumpkin seed oil and a good pinch each of salt and pepper and pulse until a chunky paste is formed. Tip into a bowl, mix with the grated cheese and set aside.

4. Line a baking sheet with baking parchment.

5. Turn out the risen dough onto a floured surface and roll it into a large rectangle, about 25 x 40cm and 1cm thick. Spread the pumpkin seed mix onto the dough, leaving a 4cm border along one long edge of the dough. Carefully roll the dough in on itself, starting at one long edge, leaving the border exposed. Brush the border with warm water then fold it over the top of the dough. Roll the bread until the border seal is underneath. Cut the roll into 12 slices and place each piece, cut side up, on the parchment-lined baking sheet. Sprinkle the remaining pumpkin seeds on top of the slices. Carefully cover the entire tray with oiled clingfilm and place somewhere warm to prove for 30 minutes.

6. Remove the clingfilm and bake the rolls for 25–30 minutes until golden and cooked through. Remove from the oven and serve warm.

Salmon Pastry

Easter Slow-cooked Leg of Lamb with Spiced Rub

May Day Spring Salad

Ultimate Veggie Barbecue

Barbecued Lamb Ribs with Chimichurri Sauce

Black Forest Gateau

Festive Season Canapés
Pork and Sage Croquettes
Quick Gin-cured Salmon with Horseradish and Parsnip
Slow-cooked Celeriac with Brie and Thyme

Stuffed Turkey Leg with Turkey Gravy

Marmalade and Earl Grey Tea-glazed Ham

Ultimate Roast Potatoes

Seasonal Sides
Caramelised Cauliflower Cheese
Green Beans with Toasted Hazelnut Butter and Anchovy
Celeriac and Parsnip Boulangère
Spiced Pumpkin Fritters

Quince, Rosemary and Honey Trifle

Mince Pie Puddings with Brandy Cream

Boxing Day Bubble and Squeak Pie

Crackling'd Slow-cooked Pork Shoulder with Baked Apple Sauce

Ham, Membrillo and Gruyère Bakes

Holiday Eats

Holiday Eats

These dishes have come about since having children. For the last 17 years we've had many different holidays, but the best have been in cottages in the UK, when we shop at local farmers' markets and in the same familiar supermarkets, then set about creating some wonderful food. I've cooked some of my loveliest dishes in a relaxed environment with my family all around me. Wherever you are, whatever you may be doing, you find yourself cooking with an open mind and a glass of wine in your hand, and you've got the best people around you. Holidays are special – we don't get many of them – and these recipes are about being relaxed and having fun with food.

Salmon Pastry

**SERVES: 4 | PREP TIME: 20 MINUTES, PLUS SALTING AND CHILLING
COOKING TIME: 25 MINUTES**

Salmon en croute is a very classic French dish which I used to make when I first started my apprenticeship at the Savoy Hotel. It had to be perfect – a crispy, flaky pastry covering a just-cooked fillet of salmon. I have slightly simplified the process here, so that less can go wrong. Instead of a whole fillet I have used fillet portions, to make individual servings. It makes a great Sunday lunch, served with salad, or a comforting supper served with steamed potatoes.

1 tsp fennel seeds
1 tsp coriander seeds
2 tbsp rock salt
½ bunch of dill, fronds finely chopped, stalks chopped
4 x 120–40g pieces of salmon, skinless and pin-boned
80g cream cheese
finely grated zest of 1 lemon
1 gherkin, finely chopped
1 tsp capers in brine, finely chopped
2 x 320g sheets of all-butter puff pastry, each cut into 4 rectangles, refrigerated
1 egg, beaten
sea salt and freshly ground black pepper

1. Put the fennel and coriander seeds in a small, dry frying pan and toast over medium heat until fragrant. Crush in a spice grinder or using a pestle and mortar then add to the rock salt and chopped dill stalks and stir. Coat the salmon pieces in the salt mixture, cover and refrigerate for 30 minutes.

2. Rinse the salt off the salmon pieces under cold running water then pat them dry with kitchen paper.

3. Mix the cream cheese, chopped dill fronds, lemon zest, gherkin and capers together in a bowl with a pinch each of salt and pepper.

4. Preheat the oven to 210°C/190°C fan/gas 7 and line a baking tray with baking parchment.

5. Lay 4 of the pastry rectangles on the lined baking tray. Divide the cream cheese mix into 4 and place a spoonful in the centre of each piece of pastry. Smooth it out, leaving a 1cm border around the edges of the pastry. Brush the borders of each pastry piece with the beaten egg.

6. Place a piece of salmon on top of the cream cheese mix, flipping the skinny end of the salmon under the fillet so that it fits well in the rectangle.

7. Take the remaining 4 pastry rectangles out of the fridge and place them on top of the salmon pieces. Using the side of your hand, carefully press the edges of the 2 pastry pieces together, to seal the salmon in. Using a fork, gently crimp a 5mm border around the edge of each parcel. Brush each parcel with beaten egg then place the entire tray in the fridge for 10 minutes.

8. Bake the salmon parcels for 20–25 minutes until golden brown. Remove from the oven, allow to rest for a few minutes then serve.

MARCUS' TIP:
This is a dish that needs to be cooked as soon as it is assembled, to avoid a 'soggy bottom' on the pastry!

Easter Slow-cooked Leg of Lamb with Spiced Rub

SERVES: 6 | PREP TIME: 15 MINUTES, PLUS MARINATING
COOKING TIME: ABOUT 2 HOURS

Lamb leg is one of my favourite joints to cook for a family roast and there's no better time to serve it than Easter. This recipe requires a little planning in advance, as the rub is best left on the lamb for at least 24 hours, so it has the chance to season the meat all the way through. The spices work really well with the aubergine, which absorbs all of the cooking juices, creating a delicious chunky sauce to serve alongside. At home we usually have lamb with buttered new potatoes.

1 bone-in leg of lamb (about 1.8kg)
   (brined for 3 hours if you wish – use 1
   quantity of the brine on page 242)
3 aubergines, quartered
1½ tbsp olive oil
½ tsp smoked paprika
½ bunch of mint, leaves chopped

FOR THE SPICE RUB
1 tsp cumin seeds
1 tsp coriander seeds
1 tsp fennel seeds
1 tsp yellow mustard seeds
3 cloves
4 green cardamom pods
leaves picked from ½ bunch of rosemary
15g table salt
25g soft dark brown sugar

1. To make the spice rub, put the cumin, coriander, fennel and mustard seeds in a small, dry frying pan with the cloves and cardamom. Toast over medium heat until fragrant, then place in a spice blender with the rosemary leaves and pulse until the mixture has a crumb-like texture (or crush using a pestle and mortar). Transfer to a bowl, add the salt and sugar and mix well.

2. Rinse the lamb and pat dry with kitchen paper, if it was brined. Gently score the skin of the lamb with criss-cross marks to create a diamond pattern then, using your hands, cover the lamb with the spice rub. Wrap the entire leg in clingfilm and refrigerate for 24–48 hours.

3. Preheat the oven to 180°C/160°C fan/gas 4.

4. Place the aubergine quarters in the bottom of a roasting tray large enough to fit the lamb. Drizzle with olive oil. Remove the clingfilm from the lamb and place it on top of the aubergines. Leave it for 30 minutes or so, to come to room temperature (if you have time), then roast for 2 hours. Check for doneness by piercing the meat with a skewer or knife to check the pinkness, and if needed, continue to roast for a further 15–30 minutes.

5. Remove the lamb leg from the oven and transfer to a serving dish. Leave in a warm place, covered with foil, to rest for 15 minutes.

6. Scrape the contents of the roasting tray into a bowl and stir in the smoked paprika and chopped mint.

7. Carve the lamb when rested and serve with the aubergines.

MARCUS' TIP:
I always prefer roasting lamb on the bone. It makes for a juicier and more tender result, and looks impressive on an Easter table.

May Day Spring Salad

SERVES: 4–6 | PREP TIME: 15 MINUTES | COOKING TIME: UNDER 5 MINUTES

Spring usually starts to make itself known at the beginning of May, meaning spring produce is under way. Green vegetables are in their prime and the short season of asparagus is always one to be celebrated. This recipe also uses new-season strawberries, to add a touch of sweetness.

2 bunches of asparagus (about 500g), tough ends trimmed and spears sliced in half diagonally
200g ripe strawberries
200g soft goats' cheese, roughly chopped
4 tbsp milk
finely grated zest and juice of 1 lemon
25ml light olive oil
2 tbsp balsamic vinegar
1 tsp wholegrain mustard
200g freshly podded peas
½ fennel bulb, thinly sliced
50g pea shoots
½ bunch of basil, leaves picked
sea salt and freshly ground black pepper

1. Bring a large pan of salted water to the boil. Blanch the asparagus for 2 minutes then drain and cool under cold running water to stop it cooking any further.

2. Hull the strawberries and cut any larger ones in half or quarters.

3. Put the goats' cheese and milk in a small blender or food processor with the lemon zest and juice and a pinch each of salt and pepper and blitz until a smooth paste is formed. Scrape it out onto a large serving bowl or platter and smooth into a circle.

4. For the dressing, mix the olive oil, balsamic vinegar and wholegrain mustard together in a bowl.

5. Place the blanched asparagus, peas, fennel, pea shoots and strawberries in a large mixing bowl and add the dressing, seasoning well with salt and pepper. Gently mix together then place on top of the goats' cheese. Finish with the basil leaves and serve.

MARCUS' TIP:
Extra virgin olive oil has the punchiest flavour and can sometimes, therefore, be a little too much when used in dressings and mayonnaises. When I do use it on its own I think of it as an ingredient in its own right, rather than just an addition.

Ultimate Veggie Barbecue

SERVES: 4 | PREP TIME: 15 MINUTES | COOKING TIME: ABOUT 15 MINUTES

We sometimes focus too much on the meat and fish elements of a barbecue – this recipe instead takes full advantage of wonderful end-of-summer vegetables. It's a great way to introduce some vegetables to a barbecue feast that people don't usually cook on the grill. You can use other produce you have to hand if you wish, such as runner beans, sugar snap peas, asparagus, aubergines and courgettes.

2 cobs of corn
1 broccoli head
1 aubergine, cut lengthways into 1cm-thick slices
50ml vegetable oil
1 bunch of spring onions
2 heads of gem lettuce, halved lengthways
sea salt and freshly ground black pepper

FOR THE HARISSA YOGHURT
2 tbsp rose harissa paste
100g Greek yoghurt
grated zest and juice of 1 lemon

FOR THE DRESSING
50ml olive oil
1 tbsp balsamic vinegar
1 tsp Dijon mustard
2 garlic cloves, finely grated
2 tbsp capers in brine, finely chopped
½ bunch of flat-leaf parsley, leaves finely chopped

1. Heat your barbecue until hot.

2. To prepare the vegetables, blanch the cobs of corn in a large pan of salted water for 2 minutes, then plunge into a bowl of iced water. Peel the tough outer layer off the broccoli stalk, quarter the head of broccoli lengthways and blanch for 2 minutes in the sweetcorn water, then plunge into iced water. When both are cold, drain and pat dry with kitchen paper. Cut the cobs of corn in half.

3. Brush the aubergine slices liberally with the vegetable oil on both sides and season with salt and pepper.

4. Place the blanched corn and broccoli in a large dish with the spring onions and gem halves. Drizzle the remaining vegetable oil over all the vegetables and season well with salt and pepper.

5. To make the harissa yoghurt, mix everything together in a bowl and season to taste with salt and pepper.

6. To make the dressing, mix everything together in a bowl and season to taste with salt and pepper.

7. To barbecue the vegetables, start with the aubergine slices, corn cobs and spring onions. Place them on the hot barbecue, turning them when charred on each side and moving them around the barbecue if some spots are hotter than others. After a few minutes, add the broccoli quarters and stalk and char. Finish with the gem lettuce – which will only take around 2 minutes on each side – then place everything on a large serving platter and drizzle firstly with the harissa yoghurt, then the dressing. Serve hot.

MARCUS' TIP:
Lettuce heads are wonderful cooked on a barbecue. You just have to be careful not to leave them on there too long – halve them, put them on quickly, then set aside to cool – and just pour a simple dressing over.

Barbecued Lamb Ribs with Chimichurri Sauce

SERVES: 4 | PREP TIME: 15 MINUTES, PLUS MARINATING
COOKING TIME: 2½ HOURS

Lamb ribs are an underused cut of meat, yet they are so delicious. They lend themselves well to slow cooking, and spicy chimichurri sauce makes a perfect fresh accompaniment. If you cannot source the ribs, you can use lamb belly, which is effectively just boneless ribs. The ribs need to be marinated in the spice rub for at least 12 hours, so therefore I tend to get started the night before I want to serve them. These are a great summer holiday barbecue dinner, and go very well with the Ultimate Veggie Barbecue (see previous page).

2 x racks of lamb ribs (around 1.5kg total)

FOR THE SPICE RUB
1 tsp cumin seeds
½ tsp fennel seeds
1 tsp onion seeds
20g table salt
25g soft dark brown sugar
5g chilli powder
1 tbsp finely chopped rosemary

FOR THE CHIMICHURRI SAUCE
½ bunch of coriander
½ bunch of flat-leaf parsley
8 mint leaves
1 green chilli, deseeded and chopped
1 garlic clove, peeled and crushed
70ml olive oil
finely grated zest and juice of 1 lime
sea salt

1. To make the spice rub, heat a dry frying pan over medium heat, add the cumin, fennel and onion seeds and toast for 4–6 minutes until fragrant. Transfer them to a spice grinder or pestle and mortar and crush to form a powder. Mix the powder with the other spice rub ingredients and coat the racks of ribs with the rub. Wrap them in clingfilm and leave to marinate in the fridge for 12 hours.

2. If you have a barbecue with a lid, heat it to low, unwrap the ribs and place them on the rack for 4 hours with the lid closed, taking care that the temperature stays around 110°C. If you are using an oven, preheat it to 150°C/130°C fan/gas 2 and place the ribs directly on the oven racks, with a tray at the bottom of the oven lined with foil to catch drips. Cook for 2½ hours then remove from the oven.

3. To make the sauce, put all ingredients into a blender or food processor (including the herb stems as well as the leaves) and pulse until a chunky paste is formed. Taste and adjust seasoning if needed. Serve with the hot ribs.

MARCUS' TIP:
I am a big fan of chimichurri sauce. It is best when made fresh and is a great accompaniment for barbecued meat, fish dishes and roasted vegetables. Mix it into a little mayonnaise to make a delicious salad dressing.

Black Forest Gateau

SERVES: 10–12 | PREP TIME: 30 MINUTES, PLUS COOLING AND CHILLING
COOKING TIME: ABOUT 50 MINUTES

This recipe is one for when you have some time on your hands and want to create a show-stopping centrepiece for a special celebration. It is a really delicious cake and makes a great pudding. I like to use black cherries in kirsch, as the syrup is very good for lightly moistening the cake and adding flavour to the cream. It might look daunting, but it's basically sponge cake with a little bit more going on. I like to pour double cream all over it, to serve.

gold dust and/or edible flowers, to finish

FOR THE FILLING

2 x 460g jars of black cherries in Luxardo, or 2 x 425g tins of black cherries
50ml kirsch
500ml double cream

FOR THE CAKE

100g soft dark brown sugar
100g caster sugar
2 eggs
160g Greek yoghurt
60g cocoa powder
120g butter, melted, plus extra for greasing
¾ tsp bicarbonate of soda
pinch of fine salt
200g plain flour
1½ tsp baking powder
160ml strong, hot coffee

FOR THE CHOCOLATE GLAZE

100ml double cream
75g dark chocolate (minimum 70% cocoa solids), cut into small pieces
50g caster sugar
25g cocoa powder, sifted

1. Preheat the oven to 170°C/150°C fan/gas 3 and grease a deep 20cm springform cake tin.

2. Put all of the cake batter ingredients in a food processor, in the order they are listed, and blitz until smooth.

3. Pour the mixture into the greased cake tin and bake for 45–50 minutes, until a skewer inserted into the middle of the cake comes out clean. Remove from the oven and allow the cake to cool in the tin, then turn it out. Cover and refrigerate for 1 hour.

4. Remove the cake from the fridge and, using a sharp serrated knife, slice into three equal layers.

5. Strain the cherries, reserving the Luxardo syrup, and cut them in half. Arrange them on the bottom and middle tiers of the cake. Mix the kirsch with the syrup from the cherries then drizzle 2 tablespoons over each cake tier. You will have some leftover liquid.

6. Whip the cream in a bowl until it forms stiff peaks, then stir in 75ml of the cherry syrup with kirsch. Divide the cream in two and spread it over the top of the cherries on the two cake layers.

7. Carefully reassemble the cake, placing the third layer on top of the first two tiers. Refrigerate while you make the glaze.

8. To make the glaze, heat 50ml of the double cream in a small saucepan (don't let it boil). Remove from the heat and pour it over the chocolate in a heatproof bowl. Leave it to sit for 5 minutes then whisk together until smooth to make a ganache. Put the remaining double cream in a small saucepan with 75ml warm water, the caster sugar and sifted cocoa powder. Bring to the boil, then strain it through a sieve over the ganache and mix well.

9. Lay a piece of clingfilm on your work surface, just larger than a wire rack. Remove the cake from the fridge and place on the wire rack. Working very gently, starting in the centre of the top of the cake and moving outwards, slowly pour the glaze over, making sure the cake is completely covered in the glaze. Place it back in the fridge for at least 1 hour for the glaze to set. You can reuse any glaze that gathered on the clingfilm under the wire rack.

10. Remove the cake from the fridge at least 2 hours before serving. Decorate with gold dust and/or edible flowers.

FESTIVE SEASON CANAPÉS

Canapés always signal a celebration to me: they are great for a pre-Christmas party, or for New Year's Eve, accompanied with some chilled champagne. This selection covers all the bases too, with canapés for for pescatarians, meat eaters and veggies.

Pork and Sage Croquettes

SERVES: 6–8 | PREP TIME: 20 MINUTES, PLUS CHILLING
COOKING TIME: ABOUT 25 MINUTES

Sausage stuffing is a crowd-pleaser in my house so I thought it only right to extend its festive appearance a little, by having it as a pre-Christmas canapé.

10g butter
½ onion, finely diced
250g sausage meat
2 tbsp finely chopped sage
25g golden raisins, finely chopped
2 tbsp finely chopped, toasted pistachio
  nuts (see page 186 for method)
vegetable oil, for deep-frying
sea salt and freshly ground black pepper

FOR THE CRUMB
30g plain flour, seasoned with salt and
  pepper
2 eggs, beaten
60g dried breadcrumbs (panko or
  homemade from old bread)

1. Heat the butter in a small frying pan over medium heat. When hot, add the onion, season well with salt and pepper and cook for about 10 minutes until lightly golden, stirring occasionally. Transfer to a mixing bowl, add the sausage meat, sage, raisins and chopped pistachio nuts. Mix well, then season with salt and pepper. Fry a little of the mix to check the seasoning, adding more salt and/or pepper if needed.

2. Roll the mixture into 16 small teaspoon-sized balls and refrigerate for at least 30 minutes.

3. While the croquettes are in the fridge, pour enough vegetable oil into a deep saucepan or deep-fat fryer to come up to about 5cm and place over a medium heat. If using a deep-fat fryer or if you have a thermometer, heat the oil to 170°C. If not, to check the oil is at the right temperature, drop a 2–3cm cube of bread into the hot oil – it should turn golden and crisp in 1 minute.

4. While the oil is heating up, put the crumb ingredients in 3 separate bowls. Coat the croquettes in the seasoned flour, then the egg and finish with a generous coating of breadcrumbs. Return to the fridge for a further 10 minutes.

5. Carefully drop a batch of croquettes in the hot oil and fry for 5–7 minutes, until cooked all the way through (a metal skewer inserted into a croquette should be hot to the touch). Lift out carefully with a slotted spoon, drain on kitchen paper and serve while hot. Repeat with the remaining croquettes.

Quick Gin-cured Salmon with Horseradish and Parsnip

SERVES: 6–8 | PREP TIME: 15 MINUTES, PLUS CURING | COOKING TIME: ABOUT 10 MINUTES

Curing salmon generally takes at least 12 hours, or up to 3 days for gravadlax. This quick-cure method still creates a great flavour, yet retains the soft flesh of the salmon. Pumpernickel is readily available nowadays, and works wonderfully well with oily fish.

10g butter
1 tbsp olive oil
2 small parsnips, peeled and grated
   (250g)
25ml milk
1 tbsp horseradish sauce
2 tbsp crème fraîche
150g piece of boneless and skinless
   salmon fillet
1 tbsp rock salt
finely grated zest of ½ orange
25ml gin
3 slices pumpernickel bread, toasted
2 tbsp finely chopped dill
sea salt and freshly ground black pepper

1. Heat the butter and olive oil in a medium saucepan over medium heat. When hot, add the grated parsnip. Season well with salt and pepper and cook for around 5 minutes until golden and soft. Add the milk and bring to a simmer for 5 minutes. Transfer the parsnip to a small blender or food processor. Add the horseradish and crème fraîche and blitz until smooth.

2. Slice the salmon as thinly as possible across the fillet (against the grain). Lay the slices in the bottom of a shallow dish. Mix the rock salt and orange zest together then rub it onto the sliced salmon. Leave to sit for 10 minutes, then add the gin and leave for a further 10 minutes. Rinse the cure off the salmon under cold running water then pat the salmon slices dry with kitchen paper.

3. Cut the pumpernickel bread into rectangles approximately 6 × 2cm. You should get around 20 slices.

4. Spread the parsnip cream onto the slices of bread. Place a piece of salmon on top and finish with the chopped dill.

Slow-cooked Celeriac with Brie and Thyme

SERVES: 6–8 | PREP TIME: 15 MINUTES | COOKING TIME: AROUND 1 HOUR 20 MINUTES

This creamy and delicious canapé is more veg-centric. You can cook the celeriac in advance, then just lightly warm it through to serve, before putting the brie on top.

1 small celeriac, peeled and halved
2 tbsp olive oil
1 tsp table salt
¼ bunch of thyme, leaves picked
3 tbsp finely chopped toasted hazelnuts
   (see page 235 for method)
100g brie

1. Preheat the oven to 180°C/160°C fan/gas 4.

2. Place the celeriac halves in a small roasting tray. Drizzle with the oil and season with the salt. Reserve 1 teaspoon of thyme leaves and scatter the rest over the celeriac. Cover the roasting tray with foil and bake for 40 minutes. Remove the foil and bake for a further 30–40 minutes, until the celeriac is tender.

3. Remove from the oven and leave until cool enough to handle. Cut the celeriac into 3cm cubes. Dip one side into the chopped hazelnuts. Slice the brie into slightly smaller pieces than the celeriac and pop a piece on top of the nut-dipped sides of the celeriac. Finish with the remaining picked thyme.

Stuffed Turkey Leg with Turkey Gravy

SERVES: 4–6 | PREP TIME: 30 MINUTES | COOKING TIME: ABOUT 2 HOURS, PLUS RESTING

I have had stuffed turkey leg at Christmas for the past ten years – I've never strayed into cooking goose or beef. Turkey leg is so much simpler and quicker to cook than a whole turkey, and needs a lot less space to cook. You can prepare everything two days in advance: roll the leg and have it ready to go in the fridge, and make the gravy beforehand so you can relax on Christmas Day.

2 boned turkey legs, approximately 1.2–1.5kg in total (brined for 2 hours if you wish – use 1 quantity of the brine on page 242)

sea salt and freshly ground black pepper

FOR THE STUFFING
50g butter
1 onion, finely diced
1 garlic clove, finely grated
200g sausage meat
1 bunch of sage, half of the leaves finely chopped
½ tsp dried marjoram

FOR THE GRAVY
turkey or chicken bones
2 tbsp vegetable oil
2 onions, cut into chunks
3 garlic cloves, peeled
2 carrots, cut into chunks
½ bunch of thyme
2 bay leaves
150ml white wine
100ml dry sherry
1 litre good-quality chicken stock
1 tsp Marmite or Bovril
1 tbsp cornflour

> **MARCUS' TIP:**
> Find a good butcher – then you can not only source great meat, but also ask them to de-bone the turkey legs for you. If you can't get turkey bones, chicken bones will suffice.

1. Start by making the gravy. Preheat the oven to 220°C/200°C fan/gas 7.

2. Put the turkey or chicken bones in a large roasting tray, put them in the oven, turn the heat down to 200°C/180°C fan/gas 6 and roast for 20–25 minutes until golden.

3. While the bones are roasting, heat a large saucepan over high heat. Add the vegetable oil. When it's almost smoking add the onions, garlic, carrots, thyme and bay leaves and brown well for about 15 minutes, stirring frequently. Add the white wine and sherry and reduce to a syrup, then add the stock, roasted bones (being sure to scrape the bottom of the roasting tray), and the unchopped sage, plus the stalks from the other half. Add the Marmite or Bovril and a good grind of black pepper and simmer gently for 1 hour. Pass through a fine sieve into a clean saucepan and simmer gently for 20 minutes. Mix the cornflour with 2 tablespoons of cold water and whisk it into the gravy. Simmer for another 10 minutes. Taste, and adjust seasoning if necessary.

4. Make the stuffing while the gravy is cooking. Melt the butter in a medium frying pan, add the onion, garlic and a generous pinch of salt and cook for 10–15 minutes until soft. Transfer to a large mixing bowl and mix in the sausage meat, finely chopped sage, marjoram and a good grind of black pepper. Fry a little spoonful in the pan to check for seasoning, adding more salt if needed.

5. Place a large piece of foil on your work surface. Working with one leg at a time, lay the boned leg on top, skin side up, and rub the skin with salt and pepper. Turn it over and place half the stuffing on the flesh side. Smooth it out with a spoon, leaving a 3cm gap at the end you are going to roll towards. Roll the leg up tightly and secure it with kitchen string, then wrap tightly in foil. Repeat with the second leg. Place in a roasting tray and roast in the oven for 25 minutes. Remove the foil and roast for another 30–35 minutes, until the skin is golden and the juices are running clear. Remove from the oven and allow to rest somewhere warm, covered loosely with foil, for 10–15 minutes. Add the roasting juices to the gravy then carve and serve.

Marmalade and Earl Grey Tea-glazed Ham

SERVES: 6–8, WITH LEFTOVERS | PREP TIME: 15 MINUTES | COOKING TIME: 2 HOURS

I very rarely cook a ham, but when I do it is so enjoyable that I wonder why I don't do it more often! I'm told by Chantelle that it is traditional to have a cooked ham on Christmas Day in New Zealand, alongside a turkey. They work really well together. The sticky, fragrant glaze on the salty ham is utterly delicious. I generally cook more ham than I need so we can use it for a few days afterwards in sandwiches, pasta dishes or my Ham, Membrillo and Gruyère Bakes (see page 243).

2–3kg middle-cut unsmoked gammon, knuckle on
1 onion, quartered
2 carrots, halved
2 celery sticks
2 bay leaves
1 tsp black peppercorns
4 cloves
4 tbsp Earl Grey tea leaves, or 8 tea bags
200g marmalade

1. Place the gammon in a large saucepan. Add the onion, carrots, celery, bay leaves, peppercorns and cloves. Cover with cold water and place over medium heat. Bring to a gentle simmer, skimming off any scum that rises to the surface, and cook for 1½ hours. Turn the heat off and allow the gammon to sit in the liquid for a further 30 minutes. Remove from the pan and leave until cool enough to handle. Strain off the liquid and keep it for soup (bearing in mind it will be rather salty).

2. Once the ham is cool enough to touch, place it on your chopping board and cut away the skin, leaving a 1cm-thick layer of fat intact on the ham. Gently score the fat with criss-cross marks to create a diamond pattern.

3. Preheat the oven to 190°C/170°C fan/gas 5 and line a roasting tray with foil.

4. Pour 100ml water into a small saucepan and bring to the boil. Add the tea leaves or bags and remove from the heat. Leave to infuse for 6 minutes then strain into a bowl. Add the marmalade to the bowl and mix well.

5. Transfer the gammon to the lined roasting tray and brush it liberally with the marmalade mix (keep a little back to use for a second glaze in the process). Place in the oven for 20 minutes, brush with the remaining glaze and return to the oven for a further 10 minutes, until the skin is crisp.

6. Remove from the oven, cover with the foil and leave to rest for 20 minutes before carving.

MARCUS' TIP:
Cloves impart a huge amount of flavour and therefore must be used sparingly. A little goes a long way – chew on one and your mouth will turn numb. Clove oil is used for toothache for that very reason!

Ultimate Roast Potatoes

SERVES: 6 | PREP TIME: 10 MINUTES, PLUS COOLING
COOKING TIME: ABOUT 1 HOUR 20 MINUTES

The perfect roast potato must have a very crispy outside and a soft, creamy inside. A good roast potato relies on using the correct potato in the first place. If they are too starchy, the natural sugars will brown before the potatoes crisp up. My dad always liked to use King Edwards for roasts, a very expensive potato. It depends on the season, but I prefer Maris Piper. I use a large amount of vegetable oil – you're semi deep-frying them. It's quite indulgent, but it does make a difference. The outside is just pure luxury and crunch.

18 potatoes, about 140g each, peeled
300g duck fat
300ml vegetable oil
½ bunch of thyme
6 garlic cloves, bashed
sea salt and freshly ground black pepper

1. Place the potatoes in a large pan of water. Season well, bring to the boil, then turn down to a simmer and cook for 18–20 minutes, until a knife inserted meets only a small amount of resistance (they shouldn't be soft all the way through). This par-boiling part of the process is crucial, as it's what makes them fluffy once you put them in a really hot tray of oil.

2. Drain the potatoes then place 4 or 5 back into the pan and cover with a lid. Shake vigorously until all edges of all potatoes have been roughed up. Repeat until all potatoes have been shaken.

3. Spread the potatoes out in a single layer on a tray. Allow to cool to help them dry out.

4. When the potatoes have cooled, preheat the oven to 240°C/220°C fan/gas 8. Remove all oven racks except the middle one, so you can have easy access to that rack.

5. Place the duck fat and vegetable oil into a deep roasting tin and place the tin in the centre of the oven for 15 minutes. Turn the heat down to 220°C/200°C fan/gas 7 then open the oven door and carefully remove the tin. Using a pair of tongs, carefully place the potatoes in the hot fat. Add the thyme and garlic and season with salt and pepper. Place the tin back in the centre of the oven and roast the potatoes for 40–50 minutes, carefully turning them every 15 minutes.

6. When the potatoes are golden, place a colander above a bowl and, using tongs, with the roasting tin still in the oven, transfer the potatoes to the colander. If you do not need to use the oven, leave the door ajar for the hot fat to cool before removing. If you do need the oven, be very careful when removing the hot fat-filled tin.

MARCUS' TIP:
Par-boiling is vital. If you put the potatoes in a roasting tray raw and cold then put them in the hot oven, the temperature of the oven will fall, and you'll lose that blast of heat required to make a great roast potato. Use vegetable oil, not olive oil, as it needs to get to a very, very high heat without burning and tasting acrid.

SEASONAL SIDES

Side dishes can add so much colour and flavour to a mealtime. The ones below are all great accompaniments for roast meats, pan-fried fish or vegetable main courses. If you want to simplify the vegetables you serve with your roast, stick to one dish and do it very well. Blanch broccoli, cauliflower, green beans, chill and put them to one side, then take them up another level: you could add fried bacon, herbs, garlic, butter. Gently warm them up in a tray in the oven with your extras just before serving and you have something really special.

Caramelised Cauliflower Cheese

SERVES: 4–6 | PREP TIME:15 MINUTES | COOKING TIME: 1 HOUR 10 MINUTES

This nutty and rich dish – which works well as a festive roast side dish or even as a main course in its own right – is a step up for cauliflower cheese, with cauliflower purée used for sauce. I like it best with the addition of smoked cheese on top, as the flavour works very well with the caramelised cauliflower.

2 medium heads cauliflower, leaves removed
100g butter
500ml milk
1 tsp Dijon mustard
2 tbsp Worcestershire sauce
1 tsp thyme leaves
50g breadcrumbs (panko or homemade from stale bread)
100g smoked Applewood cheese, grated
sea salt and freshly ground black pepper

1. Preheat the oven to 230°C/210°C fan/gas 8.

2. Cut the stem from the cauliflowers, trim and finely chop. Cut the cauliflowers into florets the size of a dessertspoon.

3. Heat half of the butter in a large saucepan over medium-high heat. Add the chopped cauliflower stems and a third of the florets. Season well with salt and cook for around 15 minutes until a dark golden colour. Add the milk, mustard and Worcestershire sauce and blitz in a blender to make a smooth purée.

4. Melt the remaining 50g of butter in a pan. Place the remaining cauliflower florets on a roasting tray. Coat with the melted butter and season with salt and pepper. Roast for 25–30 minutes, stirring regularly, until golden.

5. Mix the roasted florets into the cauliflower purée with the thyme leaves and transfer to a large (approximately 20 x 30cm) pie dish or baking dish.

6. Mix the breadcrumbs and cheese together and place on top of the cauliflower mixture.

7. Bake for 15–20 minutes until the top is golden, then remove from the oven and serve.

Green Beans with Toasted Hazelnut Butter and Anchovy

SERVES: 4–6 | PREP TIME: 10 MINUTES | COOKING TIME: AROUND 10 MINUTES

The freshness of green beans works so well with the richness of the nut butter, and the saltiness of the anchovies. If you are not an anchovy fan, you can use capers instead. This makes a wonderful summer side dish. Try it alongside the Salmon Pastry (page 206) or Easter Slow-cooked Leg of Lamb with Spiced Rub (page 208).

100g blanched hazelnuts
3½ tbsp olive oil
500g green beans, stalks removed
6–8 anchovies, roughly chopped
sea salt and freshly ground black pepper

1. Preheat the oven to 200°C/180°C fan/gas 6.

2. Place the hazelnuts in a small roasting tray and toast in the oven for 8–10 minutes until golden. Remove from the oven and allow to cool slightly, then roughly chop 20g. Put the remaining hazelnuts in a blender or food processor with the olive oil. Season well with salt and pepper and blitz until smooth.

3. To prepare the beans, blanch them in a pan of boiling water for 3–4 minutes until just tender. Drain well.

4. Place the beans in a large serving dish and drizzle over the hazelnut purée. Scatter the chopped hazelnuts and anchovies on top and finish with a good grind of black pepper.

Celeriac and Parsnip Boulangère

SERVES: 4–6 | PREP TIME: 15 MINUTES | COOKING TIME: 1 HOUR

Earthy celeriac and sweet parsnip combine in this to create a rich and tasty side dish. This makes a great accompaniment to roast chicken, a steak, the roast lamb on page 208 or even on its own with some green vegetables. Use a mandoline to thinly slice the celeriac and parsnips, if you have one.

1 celeriac, peeled, halved and sliced into
  2mm-thick slices
2 large parsnips, peeled and sliced into
  2mm-thick slices
100g butter, melted
1 tsp finely chopped rosemary
sea salt and freshly ground black pepper

1. Preheat the oven to 200°C/180°C fan/gas 6. Line a 20cm square cake tin with baking parchment.

2. Put the sliced celeriac and parsnips in a large bowl with the melted butter, rosemary and a generous pinch each of salt and pepper. Use your hands to coat the slices all over. Layer the slices in the bottom of the lined cake tin and keep layering, evenly, until you have used all of the slices. Cover the tin with foil and bake for 30 minutes. Remove the foil and bake for a further 30 minutes. Remove from the oven and serve.

Spiced Pumpkin Fritters

MAKES: 12 FRITTERS | PREP TIME: 20 MINUTES | COOKING TIME: ABOUT 1 HOUR

These make a great autumnal snack or canapé, or a side dish for turkey or pork. Try to use pumpkins that are firm fleshed and a vibrant yellow colour as they will be sweeter and drier. My favourite varieties for this purpose are delicata and kabocha.

200g peeled and deseeded pumpkin
½ tsp cumin seeds
½ tsp coriander seeds
150g plain flour
1 tsp baking powder
¼ tsp ground cinnamon
½ nutmeg, finely grated
1 egg
125ml milk
1 tbsp finely chopped coriander
vegetable oil, for deep-frying
sea salt and freshly ground black pepper

1. Preheat the oven to 200°C/180°C fan/gas 6.

2. Season the pumpkin with salt and wrap in foil. Place on a baking tray and bake for 35–40 minutes, until tender, then remove from the oven and open the foil to allow the pumpkin to cool.

3. When cool enough to touch, coarsely grate the pumpkin into a bowl.

4. Put the cumin and coriander seeds in a small, dry frying pan and toast over medium heat until fragrant. Crush using a spice grinder or pestle and mortar.

5. Sift the flour and baking powder into a bowl. Add the ground cumin and coriander seeds, cinnamon and nutmeg and stir.

6. In another bowl, beat together the egg and milk, then pour the mixture into the flour. Mix until smooth, then season with salt and pepper and mix in the grated pumpkin and chopped coriander, being careful not to over-mix (which would prevent the fritters being fluffy).

7. Pour enough vegetable oil into a deep saucepan or deep-fat fryer to come up to about 5cm and place over medium heat. If using a deep-fat fryer or if you have a thermometer, heat the oil to 170°C. If not, to check the oil is at the right temperature, drop a 2–3cm cube of bread into the hot oil – it should turn golden and crisp in 1 minute.

8. Fry 4 dessertspoonfuls of the fritter mixture for about 5 minutes, until a skewer inserted into a fritter comes out clean. Lift out carefully with a slotted spoon, drain on kitchen paper and repeat with the remaining mix (you should get 12 spoonfuls out of the mixture, so 12 fritters). Serve hot.

Masterclass ULTIMATE MASHED POTATO

Wherever you shop, the floury potatoes are likely to be labelled for function: what's a chipper, a roaster and what's good for mash. But the process is equally important when it comes to mash. It's very straightforward: cut evenly, cook evenly and don't rush. First, peel the potatoes cleanly, then wash them and cut them all into evenly sized pieces, otherwise the smaller potato pieces will overcook, and before they break they will absorb water, which will make your mash watery and tasteless. Boil them in salted water at a slow boil – a fast boil will overcook the outside before the middle of the potato chunks are cooked through; you don't want lumps of undercooked potato in your mash.

Once the potatoes are cooked all the way through, but not quite falling apart, drain and leave them for a good 5 minutes, then shake them around and put them back in the pan, off the heat. The potatoes should still be hot enough to take the butter on board. Mash to your liking – a potato ricer really does help.

There are a few things you can add at this point; hot milk, butter or even cheese or herbs. If I am glazing something, like the chicken pie on page 72 or a shepherd's pie, I use egg yolk to enrich the mashed potato. You don't need an egg yolk, but you do need tons of butter. Potatoes cooked correctly will take on more milk and more butter – for a family of four, I put anything up to three-quarters to a whole pack of butter into my mashed potato and it tastes absolutely amazing. My kids love it. (And butter is good for you, by the way.) But the key is that the potato must be able to absorb that butter. The butter is effectively an oil – it's saturated, and it can taste greasy if you don't incorporate it properly. Add the cubed cold butter and whip it up with a rubber spatula, almost aerating it. You need three parts milk to four parts potato – so if you have 600g potatoes you'll need 450ml milk.

Each time you add a bit of butter, add a bit of hot milk and repeat. Adding cold milk will cool it, which means you're back to square one and you will have to go back to the hob to reheat the potato, risking burning it at the bottom of the pan. If you're adding an egg yolk, whip it in last.

I like to season it at different stages: when boiling the potatoes, then again when adding the butter and the milk, and then again at the final taste test. The key to seasoning something well is to never to add it all at the end. Salt needs to be brought into the equation from the beginning to bring out the best flavour of the potato.

Quince, Rosemary and Honey Trifle

**SERVES: 8 | PREP TIME: 30 MINUTES, PLUS CHILLING, COOLING AND SETTING
COOKING TIME: 1¾ HOURS**

You probably associate raspberry trifle with Christmas. Delicious though they are, raspberries are most definitely not in season in December. I have therefore opted to use a fruit that is in peak season: fragrant quince. Everyone has their own interpretation of a trifle, and no one ever thinks of using quince. It's seen as an unusual fruit, and has such a unique flavour. When cooked, it turns a lovely deep shade of pinky red, so makes a perfect addition. I could eat trifle throughout the year, not just at Christmas.

250g honey
1 sprig of rosemary
2 large quince, peeled, quartered and cored (550g)
3 gelatine leaves
200g Madeira cake, diced into 2cm cubes
25ml dry sherry

FOR THE CUSTARD
150ml milk
150ml double cream
3 sprigs of rosemary
4 egg yolks
50g caster sugar
2 gelatine leaves

FOR THE CREAM
150g double cream
100g crème fraîche
finely grated zest of 1 clementine

MARCUS' TIP:
I prefer my trifle not straight from the fridge as the flavour and texture improve when it is not so cold. I therefore make all the elements up then assemble it just prior to serving.

1. Place the honey and rosemary in a medium saucepan. Add 750ml warm water, bring to the boil then reduce to a gentle simmer and add the quince. Cover and simmer for 1½ hours, until the quince are soft.

2. Strain the quince over a heatproof bowl and pour the liquid back into the saucepan. Return to the heat and simmer for a further 10–15 minutes. Pour the liquid from the saucepan into a measuring jug – you want 400ml. Return this to the pan, setting the rest aside.

3. When the quince are cool enough to touch, cut them into 2cm dice and refrigerate.

4. Soak the 3 gelatine leaves in a shallow bowl of cold water for 5 minutes.

5. Bring the 400ml of syrup to the boil. Squeeze the water from the gelatine and stir it into the hot liquid until completely dissolved. Strain into a clean, small heatproof container and refrigerate for 1–3 hours until set.

6. To make the custard, put the milk, cream and rosemary sprigs in a medium saucepan. Bring to a gentle simmer then remove from the heat. Cover with clingfilm and leave to infuse for 20 minutes. Strain, discarding the rosemary, and pour the infused milk back into the saucepan. Bring back to just below the boil, stirring frequently.

7. Put the egg yolks and sugar in a mixing bowl and whisk together. Slowly pour the hot milk mixture into the bowl, whisking as you do so.

8. Pour the mixture back into the pan and cook over very low heat, stirring continuously, until the mixture coats the back of a

wooden spoon. While the custard is cooking, soak the 2 leaves of gelatine in a shallow bowl of cold water for 5 minutes.

9. Squeeze the water from the gelatine and stir it into the hot custard until completely dissolved. Strain through a sieve, cover and chill in the fridge.

10. For the cream, whisk the cream, crème fraîche and clementine zest together in a bowl until stiff peaks form.

11. To assemble the trifle, place the quince, diced sponge and sherry in your trifle bowl along with 200ml of the reserved quince syrup (any leftovers make a great addition to a champagne cocktail or gin and tonic, by the way). Cut the quince jelly into cubes and add it to the bowl. Mix very gently. Whisk the custard then pour it on top. Finish with the cream and serve straight away or refrigerate for up to 4 hours before serving.

Mince Pie Puddings with Brandy Cream

SERVES: 6 | PREP TIME: 15 MINUTES, PLUS 3 DAYS INFUSING
COOKING TIME: 25 MINUTES

If you are not a fan of traditional heavy Christmas pudding, then this is a recipe for you. It combines the flavours of mince pies with Christmas pudding, in a lighter style. The fruit mince mix gets better the longer it marinates, so if you can do this at least 3 days in advance you will get an improved flavour in the finished puddings.

FOR THE FRUIT MINCE
1 cooking apple, grated (150g)
finely grated zest of 1 orange
20g pitted prunes, finely chopped
50ml brandy
½ whole nutmeg, grated
1 tbsp ground cinnamon
120g shop-bought Christmas mincemeat

FOR THE BRANDY CREAM
2 tbsp soft dark brown sugar
50ml brandy
150ml double cream

FOR THE PUDDING MIX
65g butter, plus extra for greasing
100g soft dark brown sugar
100g golden syrup
½ tsp ground cinnamon
½ tsp ground ginger
½ tsp ground mixed spice
60ml milk
1 egg
140g self-raising flour

1. Mix all of the fruit mince ingredients together in a bowl. Cover and refrigerate for at least 3 days.

2. To make the brandy cream, put the sugar and brandy in a small saucepan and place over low heat. Heat until the sugar has dissolved then remove from the heat and allow to cool. When cool, whisk it into the cream gently, just to combine. Cover and refrigerate.

3. Preheat the oven to 190°C/170°C fan/gas 5. Grease 6 pudding ramekins and set them on a baking tray.

4. To make the pudding mix, place the butter, dark brown sugar, golden syrup and spices in a small saucepan over low heat. When the butter begins to melt, stir until all of the butter has melted. Remove from the heat and transfer to a mixing bowl. Add the milk and egg. Mix. Gently fold in the flour, taking care not to over-mix.

5. Divide the fruit mince evenly among the ramekins then top with the pudding mix. Bake for 20–25 minutes, until a skewer inserted into the puddings comes out clean.

6. Serve the puddings warm, with the brandy cream drizzled over the top.

Boxing Day Bubble and Squeak Pie

SERVES: 6 | PREP TIME: 15 MINUTES | COOKING TIME: 1 HOUR

Bubble and squeak is a really traditional dish to serve the day after a roast, and a great way to use up any leftovers. Use this recipe as a guide, as you may have different vegetables, or meat, left over from Christmas Day or your Sunday roast, so add it all in. I like to serve this with cranberry sauce and gravy on the side.

60g butter

2 onions, thinly sliced

6 tbsp vegetable oil

500g roast potatoes, sweet potato, pumpkin or celeriac, diced

200g cooked Brussels sprouts, chopped

300g cooked meat (turkey, ham or beef), diced

100g gravy

6 sheets of filo pastry

1 tbsp onion seeds

sea salt and freshly ground black pepper

MARCUS' TIP:
Onions have a natural sweetness, which is only found when you cook them slowly in a covered pan. Sweating an onion slowly brings out its real core flavour. You need to have patience.

1. Preheat the oven to 200°C/180°C fan/gas 6.

2. In a large frying pan, heat 30g of the butter over medium heat. When hot, add the onions, season with salt and cook for 20–25 minutes until golden. Remove from the pan, transfer to a large bowl and set aside. Clean the pan.

3. Put 3 tablespoons of the vegetable oil in the frying pan and heat over high heat. When hot, add the cooked potatoes (or other veg you are using). Season with salt and pepper and cook for about 5 minutes, until crispy. Add them to the onions. Repeat the process with the remaining oil, cooking the sprouts then the meat for about 5 minutes each until crispy. Add to the potatoes and onions.

4. Add the gravy to the bowl of cooked leftovers and gently mix through. Transfer to a pie dish, around 26cm in diameter.

5. Melt the remaining butter and use it to brush each sheet of the filo pastry. Lightly scrunch each sheet of pastry and place on top of the bubble and squeak. Sprinkle with the onion seeds then bake for 20–25 minutes until the pastry is golden. Remove from the oven and serve.

Crackling'd Slow-cooked Pork Shoulder with Baked Apple Sauce

**SERVES: 6 | PREP TIME: 15 MINUTES, PLUS BRINING AND RESTING
COOKING TIME: ABOUT 2 HOURS**

In my last book, *New Classics*, I included a section on brining, and why I use the technique as often as I do. The main benefits of it are that firstly, it seasons the ingredient all the way through, rather than just on the surface. Secondly, it tenderises the meat. I have brined the pork shoulder here, which needs 12 hours in the brine, so get ahead and start it the day before you want to serve the dish. The rock salt draws out the moisture in the skin, ensuring crispy crackling. We generally have roast pork on New Year's Day and this is the perfect winter warmer.

1 boned and rolled pork shoulder (about 1.4kg), skin finely scored (you can ask your butcher to do this)
1 tbsp rock salt
1 onion, quartered
3 cooking apples, cored and quartered (650g)
¼ bunch of thyme
½ nutmeg, finely grated
200ml good-quality vegetable or chicken stock
2 tbsp honey
100–200ml apple juice
freshly ground black pepper

FOR THE BRINE
140g table salt
½ tsp white peppercorns
½ tsp coriander seeds
½ tsp fennel seeds
6 sprigs of thyme
2 bay leaves

MARCUS' TIP:
When carving meat with a crispy skin, such as pork or duck, slice from the underside so the skin is sliced last. You will get a cleaner cut.

1. To make the brine, put all of the ingredients in a medium-large saucepan, with 500ml water. Place over high heat and bring to the boil to dissolve the salt, then remove from the heat and add 1.5 litres of cold water. Allow to cool.

2. Place the pork shoulder in a large container and pour the cooled brine over the top, ensuring the shoulder is fully submerged. Cover and refrigerate for 12 hours.

3. Remove the pork from the brine and pat it dry with kitchen paper. Place the shoulder on a wire rack, sprinkle the scored skin with the rock salt and rub it in really thoroughly. Leave it out of the fridge for 1½ hours before roasting, to allow it to come to room temperature.

4. Preheat the oven to 230°C/210°C fan/gas 8.

5. Place the onion, apples (skin on), thyme, nutmeg and a good grind of black pepper in a roasting tray large enough to fit the pork. Add the stock, place the pork on top, skin side up, then put in the oven and roast for 35 minutes.

6. Turn the heat down to 170°C/150°C fan/gas 4 and cook for a further 1½ hours. Remove from the oven and carefully transfer the pork from the roasting tray into a dish. Cover loosely with foil and leave to rest for 20 minutes.

7. Remove the thyme stalks from the roasting tray then scrape the onion and apple into a blender or food processor. Add the honey and 100ml of the apple juice. Blitz until smooth, adding more apple juice if needed. Keep somewhere warm.

8. Remove the string from the pork and carve, using a very sharp knife. Serve with the apple sauce.

Ham, Membrillo and Gruyère Bakes

SERVES: 4 | PREP TIME: 15 MINUTES, PLUS CHILLING
COOKING TIME: 20 MINUTES

These make a great canapé as well as an addition to a lunch or supper dish. You can make them and freeze them ahead, baking them in a hot oven when you're ready to serve. They are also a great way to use up any cheese and ham left from Christmas! Membrillo, a quince paste, is the perfect accompaniment to cheese – its sweetness complements the salty creaminess very well.

320g flaky puff pastry sheet
1 tbsp wholegrain mustard
4 tbsp cream cheese
20g membrillo
4 slices of cooked ham
90g Gruyère cheese, grated
1 egg, beaten
freshly ground black pepper

1. Line a baking tray with baking parchment.

2. Cut the puff pastry into 8 rectangles, 4 slightly larger than the other 4. Refrigerate.

3. Mix the mustard and cream cheese together in a bowl with a good grind of black pepper.

4. Place the smaller pastry rectangles on the lined baking tray. Spread the membrillo on the base of each, leaving a 1cm border around the edges of the pastry. Place the ham on top, then cover with the mustard mix. Top with the grated Gruyère, leaving the border intact.

5. Take the remaining larger pastry rectangles out of the fridge and score 6 small horizontal lines in each one. Brush the borders of the topped pastry rectangles with the beaten egg. Place one of the scored pastry pieces on top of each one. Using the side of your hand, carefully press the edges of the 2 pastry pieces together, to seal the filling in. Brush the top of each parcel with beaten egg then place the entire tray in the fridge for 10 minutes.

6. When ready to bake, preheat the oven to 210°C/190°C fan/gas 7. Bake the parcels for 15–20 minutes until golden, then serve warm.

MARCUS' TIP:
I generally have a few 'cooking' cheeses in my fridge. Cheddar, for a milder, kid-friendly cheese, then also Gruyère and smoked Applewood or Monterey Jack. Gruyère has a sweeter flavour and the latter two, a lovely smokiness.

Cured Salmon with Buttermilk, Bergamot and Kohlrabi

Asparagus with Brown Butter Hollandaise, Hazelnut Crumb and Poached Egg

Spice-roasted Quail with Freekeh, Pistachio and Lime Pickle

Confit Duck Ravioli with Cucumber and a Peanut, Sesame and Chilli Dressing

Lemon Sole with Brown Crab, Aioli and Samphire

Whole Roast Monkfish Tail with Mushrooms and Thyme

Parmesan, Oregano and Onion Baked Pumpkin

Aromatic Aubergine with Cashew and Turmeric Sauce

Rack of Lamb with Lamb and Harissa Ragu and Courgette

Lamb Hotpot

'Nduja-stuffed Pork with Smoked Bacon and Red Wine Sauce

Port-braised Feather Blade Steaks with Potato, Onion and Horseradish Gratin

Tarts

Milk Chocolate, Raspberry and Thyme Tart

Fig and Hazelnut Tarts with Smoky Crème Fraîche

Burnt Honey Parfait with White Chocolate and Apricot

Pear and Star Anise Tarte Tatin with Buttermilk Ice Cream

Weekend Dining

Weekend Dining

This is about sharing food with friends and family. I find it fascinating how differently people do weekend dining. Whether it's for entertaining friends or just showing off to your family, these times are about taking your food up a notch, putting in a little extra effort and planning but still enjoying the process. The recipes are more daring, and there are techniques running through them that are there to improve your skills as a chef and cook, and give you a little bit more understanding about the mystery of food. It's about stepping out of your working life and preparing food with a sense of occasion.

Cured Salmon with Buttermilk, Bergamot and Kohlrabi

SERVES: 4 AS A STARTER | PREP TIME: 20 MINUTES, PLUS CURING AND STRAINING

Bergamot is an Italian citrus fruit that comes into season at the end of autumn. It has a wonderful perfume, and tastes like a cross between a lime, grapefruit and lychee. The zest and juice makes for something a little different. If they are not available, a lime will work just as well. Kohlrabi is a rather underrated vegetable which lends a delicious freshness and crunch to any dish. The salmon needs to cure for 8 hours for the best flavour, so organisation is key with this dish!

1 bunch of dill, finely chopped

finely grated zest of 1 lemon

50g rock salt

25g demerara sugar

8 juniper berries, crushed

1 piece of salmon fillet, skinless and pin-boned (about 350g)

150g buttermilk

finely grated zest and juice of 1 small (or ½ large) bergamot

2 tbsp olive oil

1 tsp honey

½ tsp creamed horseradish

2 kohlrabi, peeled and thinly sliced

sea salt and freshly ground black pepper

1. Combine three-quarters of the chopped dill with the lemon zest, rock salt, demerara sugar and crushed juniper berries in a bowl. Put the salmon in a small dish and pack the cure in and around it. Cover the dish loosely with clingfilm and refrigerate for 8 hours.

2. While the fish is curing, line a sieve with a piece of clean muslin or thick kitchen paper and place over a bowl. Put the buttermilk in the sieve and put the bowl in the fridge for 6 hours. Scrape the strained buttermilk out of the muslin cloth or kitchen paper, put it into a clean bowl and whisk to loosen it.

3. When the salmon is cured, remove the cure and rinse the salmon under cold running water. Pat dry with kitchen paper and slice the fish thinly.

4. Mix the bergamot zest and juice together with the olive oil, honey and horseradish. Mix this into the sliced kohlrabi in a bowl and season with salt and pepper.

5. Serve the sliced salmon with a spoonful of the whisked buttermilk and the kohlrabi, finishing with the remaining dill.

MARCUS' TIP:
Only eat raw salmon or tuna when it's very fresh. Go to a good fishmonger to source your fish and you'll always be fine. Be brave and have a go.

Asparagus with Brown Butter Hollandaise, Hazelnut Crumb and Poached Egg

SERVES: 4 AS A STARTER | PREP TIME: 30 MINUTES | COOKING TIME: ABOUT 30 MINUTES

Making hollandaise seems to be one of those things that scares a lot of people. The trick to it is to get the temperature of all your ingredients correct, and to take your time. This recipe uses brown butter, which gives it a lovely, nutty flavour.

30g butter, cubed
100g blanched hazelnuts
2 slices of sourdough (about 100g), torn into small pieces
4 eggs
¼ tsp white vinegar
2 bunches of asparagus (about 500g), tough ends trimmed
sea salt and freshly ground black pepper

FOR THE HOLLANDAISE
2 shallots, peeled and sliced
100ml white wine
1 bay leaf
3 sprigs of thyme
40ml white wine vinegar
¼ tsp fennel seeds
250g butter, cubed
3 egg yolks

MARCUS' TIP:
The freshness of the egg is the most important thing here. You can put a little bit of acid in the water, and you can season it, but at the end of the day, you're just dropping an egg into a pan of water, and if it doesn't hold together it is because your egg is too old. For those who want that perfect poached egg shape, buy poached egg moulds.

1. To make the hollandaise reduction, put the shallots, wine, herbs, vinegar and fennel seeds in a saucepan and bring to the boil. Cook for 6–8 minutes until reduced to a third, then strain into a jug and discard the shallots and herbs.

2. Preheat the oven to 200°C/180°C fan/gas 6.

3. Put the butter in a small roasting dish with the hazelnuts and sourdough. Season lightly and bake for 10–15 minutes, stirring halfway, until golden. Remove, allow to cool, then roughly chop.

4. To poach the eggs, bring a large saucepan of water to the boil and add a heavy pinch of salt. Crack the eggs into four bowls, adding a few drops of vinegar to each. Whisk the boiling water so it swirls in a whirlpool, turn the heat down to a gentle simmer then slide in the eggs. Poach for 3–4 minutes, remove with a slotted spoon and place on a warm plate. Keep warm.

5. For the hollandaise, begin by making the brown butter. Place the butter in a medium saucepan over medium-high heat. When it has melted and is foaming, whisk it quickly to form a deep brown butter. Immediately remove from the heat and strain through a fine sieve into a jug. Cool until warm to the touch.

6. Place the egg yolks in a large stainless steel or heatproof glass bowl. Bring a third of a pan of water to a very gentle simmer. Place the bowl of egg yolks over the pan and whisk by hand until they are thick and ribbons form when you lift the whisk. Very slowly add a little of the brown butter, whisking continuously. Keep adding small amounts of the butter, whisking well between additions, then when the hollandaise begins to thicken, add 1 tablespoon of the reduction, whisk again, add another tablespoon, whisk until smooth, then continue adding the butter. Add more reduction if needed. Season with sea salt.

7. Bring a large pan of salted water to the boil. Blanch the asparagus for 3 minutes. Drain and divide the asparagus among 4 warm plates. Top with a poached egg and hollandaise. Finish with the hazelnut crumb and serve while hot.

Spice-roasted Quail with Freekeh, Pistachio and Lime Pickle

SERVES: 4 AS A STARTER | PREP TIME: 30 MINUTES, PLUS MARINATING
COOKING TIME: ABOUT 1½ HOURS

This show-off dish makes a fantastic starter at any time of year. If you want to turn it into a more substantial main course, you can use poussin in place of the quail. The lime pickle makes more than you will need, but it is a delicious chutney to have in the fridge to serve with cold meats, curries or fish. People are often nervous of quail as they see it as a little bird with a gamey flavour that's a pain to cook, but actually it's not. It's really delicious and doesn't have any gaminess at all.

4 quail (brined for 2 hours if you wish –
  use 1 quantity of the brine on page 242)
80g freekeh
20g golden or plain raisins
1 tbsp toasted sesame oil
50g shelled unsalted pistachios, roughly
  chopped
4 tbsp Greek yoghurt
1 tbsp finely chopped coriander leaves
1 tbsp finely chopped mint leaves
sea salt and freshly ground black pepper

FOR THE LIME PICKLE
4 unwaxed limes, washed and finely diced
  (skin included)
½ tsp table salt
1 tbsp vegetable oil
1 tsp black mustard seeds
2cm piece of fresh ginger, peeled and
  finely grated
1 garlic clove, finely grated
1 green chilli, deseeded and finely diced
75g soft light brown sugar
2 tbsp white wine vinegar

FOR THE SPICE MIX
½ tsp fennel seeds
½ tsp cumin seeds
4 green cardamom pods, bashed
½ tsp ground cinnamon
½ tsp soft dark brown sugar
2 tbsp vegetable oil
½ tsp table salt

1. To make the lime pickle, toss the lime pieces in the salt and set aside for 30 minutes. Heat the vegetable oil in a medium saucepan over medium heat. When hot, add the mustard seeds. When they start to pop, add the ginger, garlic and chilli. Fry for 2 minutes then add the salted lime, sugar and vinegar. Add 100ml warm water, cover and bring to a gentle simmer, stirring regularly. Simmer for 1 hour, until the limes are soft, then remove from the heat and set aside to cool.

2. For the spice mix, put the fennel and cumin seeds and cardamom pods in a small frying pan over medium-high heat. Toast until fragrant then, using a spice grinder or pestle and mortar, grind to a powder. Add the remaining ingredients and mix well.

3. Rub the spice mix over the quail and wrap each one tightly in clingfilm. Leave to marinate in the fridge for 1 hour.

4. Remove the quail from the fridge to come to room temperature and preheat the oven to 220°C/200°C fan/gas 7.

5. Cook the freekeh according to the packet instructions. Add the raisins for the last 5 minutes of cooking. Drain well, add the sesame oil and pistachios and mix through.

6. While the freekeh is cooking, remove the clingfilm from the quail and sit them in a roasting dish. Place in the oven for 10 minutes, then turn the heat down to 180°C/160°C fan/gas 4. Cook for a further 10 minutes. Remove from the oven, cover with foil and leave to rest for 10 minutes before serving.

7. Mix the yoghurt with the herbs and a pinch of salt and pepper.

8. Serve the quail with the freekeh, lime pickle and yoghurt.

Confit Duck Ravioli with Cucumber and a Peanut, Sesame and Chilli Dressing

SERVES: 2 AS A STARTER, 3 AS A MAIN | PREP TIME: 1¾ HOURS, PLUS SALTING, COOLING AND CHILLING | COOKING TIME: ABOUT 3¾ HOURS

The time it takes to make this dish is somewhat in your hands. Given the availability of good-quality shop-bought ingredients, you can skip some of the steps that take up a little more time, if you wish. Instead of buying raw duck legs, pick up some confit duck legs in the chilled section, or in a can. And if you prefer not to make pasta from scratch, buy gyoza wrappers instead. If you are making the duck confit, start the day before you want to serve the dish, as the legs need to be salted for a good eight hours, and if you are making the pasta dough from scratch, you will need a pasta machine.

4 skin-on duck legs

100g rock salt

500g duck fat

3 tbsp dark soy sauce or tamari

2 tbsp plum sauce

½ bunch of coriander, finely chopped (leaves and stalks)

50ml white wine vinegar

½ cucumber, halved lengthways, seedy centre removed, then flesh diced

20g unsalted toasted peanuts, finely chopped (see page 186 for method)

FOR THE PASTA

275g '00' pasta flour, plus extra for dusting

1 tsp sea salt

2 large eggs, plus 4 large egg yolks

1 tbsp olive oil

MARCUS' TIP:
'00' flour is an Italian grade of flour that makes a silkier pasta dough than English plain or bread flour. It has a finer texture and also a lower protein content, giving it a certain elasticity too, which is perfect for making into pasta.

1. Start by confiting the duck. Lay the duck legs, skin side up, in a shallow bowl or tray. Sprinkle over the rock salt and leave in the fridge for 8–12 hours.

2. Rinse the salt from the duck legs and pat them dry with kitchen paper.

3. Preheat the oven to 150°C/130°C fan/gas 2.

4. Heat the duck fat in a 20cm square roasting tray in the oven until melted. Add the duck legs, ensuring they are submerged in the fat. Cover the tray with foil and cook slowly in the oven for 3–3½ hours until the duck is tender and you can put a butter knife through the flesh easily. Remove from the oven and allow to cool slightly, then carefully remove from the fat. Pick the meat from the bones and place it into a mixing bowl, discarding the bones and skin. Add the soy sauce, plum sauce and coriander and mix well. Add 4 tablespoons of the duck fat and mix to combine. Shape the mix into 12 balls, place on a plate, cover and refrigerate.

5. While the duck legs are cooking, make the pasta. Put the flour and salt in a food processor. In a jug, beat together the whole eggs and 2 of the egg yolks. Pour about a third of the egg mixture into the food processor. Pulse to combine then, with the motor running, add the oil. Slowly pour in some more egg mixture to get a coarse, crumbly texture. Use your hands to squeeze a small amount of the mixture; if it doesn't come together well, add a little more egg.

RECIPE CONTINUES OVER THE PAGE

FOR THE PEANUT, SESAME AND CHILLI DRESSING

25g caster sugar

1 tbsp fish sauce

25ml rice wine vinegar

1 green chilli, deseeded and finely diced

100ml toasted sesame oil

60g unsalted toasted peanuts, finely chopped (see page 186 for method)

10g white sesame seeds, toasted (see page 190 for method)

10g black sesame seeds

6. Turn the dough out onto a lightly floured work surface. It will be crumbly, but start to bring it together to form a soft ball. Knead well until it is smooth, silky and matt in texture. Wrap the dough in clingfilm and leave to rest in the fridge for at least 1 hour.

7. While the pasta is resting, make the dressing. Put the caster sugar, fish sauce and rice wine vinegar in a small saucepan, bring to the boil and cook for 5 minutes. Add the chilli and cook for another 2 minutes. Add the remaining ingredients and remove from the heat. Allow to sit.

8. In a separate small saucepan, bring the white wine vinegar to a simmer. Pour it over the cucumber and refrigerate.

9. Once the pasta dough has rested it is ready to roll. Divide it into quarters. Working with one piece at a time, roll each piece into a strip that is roughly the same width as your pasta machine. Lightly dust the dough and machine with flour and roll each one through the machine. Start with the thickest setting and work your way down to the second thinnest setting, sprinkling with flour as you go. Repeat running the pasta through the machine on each setting 2–3 times until you have very smooth, thin and even sheets of pasta. Repeat with the remaining pieces of dough.

10. Cut out 24 circles of pasta (each sheet should give you 6 circles), using a 10cm ring cutter or a sharp knife and cutting around a circular shape (such as a tea cup or mug).

11. Lay 6 discs on your work surface and cover the remaining discs with clingfilm. Brush the egg yolk (from the remaining 2 yolks, mixed together) around 1cm of the edge of each disc then place a duck confit ball in the centre. Place a disc of pasta on top then press down around the filling first to remove any air trapped inside and then press down around the edges to seal. Continue with the remaining pasta discs until you have 12 ravioli.

12. Bring a large pan of salted water to the boil. Reduce to a rapid simmer. Carefully cook the raviolis, in 2 batches, for 7–9 minutes. Remove from the water using a slotted spoon and place in a colander to drain. Place 2 or 3 ravioli on each plate, then then top with the cucumber, chopped peanuts and the dressing.

Lemon Sole with Brown Crab, Aioli and Samphire

SERVES: 4 | PREP TIME: 15 MINUTES | COOKING TIME: UNDER 15 MINUTES

Always ensure you purchase your lemon sole skinless, as it is quite a job to remove the skin. It's great cooked on the bone – you wouldn't want it cooked any other way. Brown crab has a lovely earthy flavour, so pairs well with the buttery taste and texture of the fish, and it brings the ocean back to the fish. The naturally salty samphire works well, but if it's unavailable, use dulse seaweed, or simply watercress. Serve with crispy potatoes or a garden salad.

4 skinless lemon sole (350–400g each)
80g butter
juice of 2 lemons
90g samphire
sea salt
boiled new potatoes, to serve
lemon wedges, to serve

FOR THE BROWN CRAB AIOLI

75g brown crab meat
1 garlic clove, finely grated
1 egg yolk
1 tbsp white wine vinegar
½ tsp Dijon mustard
pinch of cayenne pepper
finely grated zest of 1 lemon
200ml olive oil

1. First, make the aioli. Place the brown crab meat and garlic in a blender or food processor and blitz until smooth. Add the egg yolk, vinegar, mustard, cayenne pepper and lemon zest and blitz for a further minute. With the motor running (if your blender or processor has a lid with a hole to pour liquids in) gradually drizzle in the oil. If necessary, remove the lid, drizzle in a little oil and blend, and repeat the process, until thick. Season to taste with salt.

2. Preheat the oven to 200°C/180°C fan/gas 6 and prepare a foil-covered roasting dish large enough to fit all 4 fish.

3. To cook the fish, you will need a large non-stick frying pan. Season the fish on both sides with salt. Place a quarter of the butter in the pan over high heat. When the butter starts to brown, gently add one of the fish to the pan. Cook for about 2 minutes until golden brown then turn it over and brown the other side for 1 minute. Gently place in the prepared roasting dish and pour the butter over the top. Repeat with the other fish and the rest of the butter.

4. Drizzle the lemon juice over the fish and place the roasting dish in the oven for 6–8 minutes, until the fish easily comes away from the bone.

5. While the fish is in the oven, bring a medium saucepan of water to the boil. Drop in the samphire and blanch for 1 minute then strain and place back in the pan.

6. When the fish come out of the oven, carefully transfer them to hot plates. Tip the cooking juices from the roasting tray into the samphire pan then spoon the samphire and juices over the fish. Serve with a large dollop of aioli and some potatoes or salad.

Whole Roast Monkfish Tail
with Mushrooms and Thyme

SERVES: 4 | PREPARATION TIME: 15 MINUTES | COOKING TIME: 45 MINUTES

Monkfish is a great fish as it has only one large bone right down the centre, so there are no fiddly pin bones to deal with. Plus, it has such a delicate flesh so really does not need much doing to it. It makes a stunning centrepiece for a dinner with friends and family, and is easily one of my favourite dishes in the book. Cooking the fish whole, on the bone, means it retains its moisture and flavour. A potato gratin makes a lovely accompaniment. This sauce works very well with all white fish – try it with sea bass, cod or haddock.

50g butter
1 monkfish tail, skin and membrane
    removed (1.5–2kg) or 2 smaller tails
    (750–1kg each)
juice of 1 lemon
400g flat mushrooms, stalks removed,
    caps thinly sliced
200g chestnut mushrooms, stalks
    removed, caps thinly sliced
sea salt and freshly ground black pepper

FOR THE SAUCE
2 tbsp vegetable oil
3 shallots, peeled and sliced
1 garlic clove, sliced
100ml Madeira wine
375ml good-quality chicken stock
¼ bunch of thyme, tied with a string
10g dried porcini mushrooms
50ml double cream

1. Preheat the oven to 150°C/130°C fan/gas 2.

2. Start by making the sauce. Heat half of the vegetable oil in a medium saucepan over medium heat. When hot, add the shallots, garlic and a pinch each of salt and pepper and cook for about 7 minutes until soft. Add the Madeira and simmer for 5–7 minutes until it has a syrupy consistency, then add the stock, thyme and dried porcini mushrooms and simmer gently for 30 minutes. Remove the thyme stalks and transfer the sauce to a blender or food processor. Blitz until smooth, pass through a fine sieve into a clean saucepan and add the cream. Keep warm until ready to serve.

3. While the sauce is simmering, heat the butter in a frying pan large enough to fit the monkfish tail(s) over high heat. Once it's foaming, season the monkfish liberally with salt then place into the hot butter. Brown the tail(s) all over for about 5 minutes in total then transfer to a roasting dish. Pour the butter over the top and place in the oven for 25 minutes. Turn the tail(s) over and cook for a further 25 minutes. Remove from the oven, cover with foil and leave to rest for 10 minutes. Turn the heat on the oven up to 220°C/200°C fan/gas 7. Squeeze the lemon juice over the monkfish and place back in the oven for 8 minutes.

4. Meanwhile, heat the remaining tablespoon of vegetable oil in a separate large frying pan. When hot, add the mushrooms, season well and cook over high heat for about 10 minutes (you might have to do this in batches, to avoid overcrowding the pan).

5. Carve the monkfish either by using a serrated knife, and cutting across the bone, or by slicing down either side of the bone and portion accordingly. Serve the monkfish fillets atop the mushrooms and smother with the mushroom sauce.

Parmesan, Oregano and Onion Baked Pumpkin

SERVES: 4 | PREP TIME: 10 MINUTES | COOKING TIME: 1 HOUR 20 MINUTES

Roasting pumpkins whole is a great way to use the entire vegetable, and it gives you a little time to do other things while dinner is cooking. I have used freekeh in this recipe, as it provides a lovely nuttiness and texture to the finished dish, but you can substitute brown rice or barley for a similar outcome. It's a great showstopper, but it's actually pretty simple to make – you put your ingredients in, you bake it. Fantastic!

100g freekeh
60g butter
2 onions, thinly sliced
½ nutmeg, finely grated
100g kale, tough stems removed and
   leaves thinly sliced
100g fresh breadcrumbs
½ bunch of oregano, leaves picked
100g Parmesan cheese, grated
1 delica pumpkin, or kabocha squash, top
   removed and seeds scooped out
sea salt and freshly ground black pepper

1. Preheat the oven to 200°C/180°C fan/gas 6.

2. Cook the freekeh according to the packet instructions. Drain well.

3. Melt 45g of the butter in a large frying pan over medium-high heat, add the onions and nutmeg, season well with salt and pepper and cook for about 15 minutes until golden, stirring frequently. Add the kale and cook for a further 3–4 minutes, until soft.

4. Put the onion mixture in a bowl and add the cooked freekeh, breadcrumbs, oregano and Parmesan. Season well with salt and pepper and stuff inside the pumpkin, replacing the 'top'. Place in a roasting tray. Melt the remaining butter and brush it over the outside of the pumpkin, again seasoning it well with salt and pepper. Bake in the oven for 1 hour, until the pumpkin is cooked through.

5. Remove from the oven, quarter the pumpkin and serve.

MARCUS' TIP:
Instead of discarding pumpkin seeds and the unwanted flesh that surrounds the seeds, place all of this in a saucepan and cover with water. Bring to the boil, then simmer for an hour or two and you can create a stock to use in soups.

Aromatic Aubergine with Cashew and Turmeric Sauce

SERVES: 4 | PREPARATION TIME: 20 MINUTES, PLUS COOLING | COOKING TIME: 55 MINUTES

This is a more involved aubergine recipe than you are probably used to. It involves cooking the aubergine whole, in an aromatic broth, then pressing and chilling it. It is then sliced and pan-fried, creating a caramelised outside and an unctuous inside. The sauce alone is a handy one to have in your repertoire, as it is quick to put together and can form the base of a curry or to serve alongside other vegetables, meat or fish.

4 tbsp vegetable oil
1 onion, halved
1 garlic clove, finely grated
2 tbsp white miso paste
2 tbsp hoisin sauce
1 tsp sriracha sauce
2 star anise
3 aubergines

FOR THE CASHEW AND TURMERIC SAUCE
2 tbsp vegetable oil
2 shallots, peeled and sliced
3cm piece of fresh ginger, peeled and
    sliced
2 small pieces of fresh turmeric, bashed
20g toasted cashew nuts (see page 132 for
    method)
¼ bunch of coriander stalks
1 x 400ml tin coconut milk
sea salt

1. Heat 1 tablespoon of the vegetable oil in a saucepan large enough to fit the whole aubergines over medium heat. When hot, add the onion and cook for 10–15 minutes until dark brown. Add the garlic and cook for 1 minute, then add the miso paste, hoisin and sriracha sauces and star anise. Add 2 litres of warm water and bring to the boil. Meanwhile, using a skewer, prick 12 holes in each aubergine, from the top to the bottom, so they run the whole way through the aubergines.

2. Turn the cooking liquor down to a simmer and add the aubergines, ensuring they are submerged in the liquid. If not, add a little more water. Weigh the aubergines down with a heatproof plate that fits inside the saucepan. Cover the saucepan and leave over low heat for 25 minutes, until the aubergines are tender.

3. Transfer the aubergines and cooking liquor to a large rectangular dish. Weigh them down again heavily and refrigerate until cold.

4. Remove from the fridge and take the aubergines out of the cooking liquor. Pour the liquor into a clean saucepan and bring to a boil to reduce by three quarters, so you have a rich glaze. Cut the aubergines in half lengthways.

5. Preheat the oven to 220°C/200°C fan/gas 7.

6. Heat another tablespoon of the vegetable oil in a large frying pan over medium-high heat. When hot, add as many aubergine slices as you can fit in the pan. Brown them for 3–5 minutes on each side, then place in a roasting tray. Repeat with the remaining oil and aubergine slices. Pour the reduced cooking liquor over the aubergines and place in the oven for 10 minutes.

7. To make the cashew and turmeric sauce, heat the vegetable oil in a medium saucepan over medium heat. When hot, add all ingredients apart from the coconut milk. Season well with salt. Cook for 10 minutes until lightly coloured then add the coconut milk. Simmer for 20 minutes, then place in a blender or food processor and blitz until smooth.

8. Serve the aubergine with the sauce and your choice of greens or brown rice on the side.

Rack of Lamb with Lamb and Harissa Ragu and Courgette

SERVES: 4 | PREPARATION TIME: 15 MINUTES | COOKING TIME: ABOUT 1 HOUR

Most of the flavour in lamb comes from the fat, so when preparing and cooking it, it's important to ensure there is enough fat attached to the meat to keep it juicy and flavoursome. Serve the lamb and ragu with buttered orzo or mash. The ragu is delicious in its own right, too – try it with pasta as a lamb Bolognese-style dish.

2 tbsp vegetable oil

2 French-trimmed racks of lamb (6–7 bones per rack) (brined for 2 hours if you wish – use 1 quantity of the brine on page 242)

25g butter, cubed

4 courgettes

1 tbsp olive oil

25g Parmesan cheese, grated

½ bunch of basil

sea salt and freshly ground black pepper

FOR THE LAMB AND HARISSA RAGU

1 tbsp vegetable oil

1 onion, finely diced

1 garlic clove, finely grated

200g lamb mince

1 tbsp tomato purée

¼ tsp sweet smoked paprika

1 tbsp rose harissa paste

¼ tsp yellow mustard seeds

¼ tsp coriander seeds

¼ tsp ras el hanout

20ml sherry vinegar

½ tbsp black treacle

1. To make the lamb and harissa ragu, heat a medium saucepan over medium heat. Add the vegetable oil and when hot, add the onion and garlic, seasoning well with salt. Cook for 10 minutes, until soft, then add the lamb mince and mix well, breaking up the mince. Add the tomato purée and cook for 10 minutes, stirring regularly, then add the remaining ingredients and cook over low heat for about 5 minutes until most of the liquid has evaporated.

2. Preheat the oven to 200°C/180°C fan/gas 6.

3. Bring the rack of lamb to room temperature (rinsing off the brine and patting dry with kitchen paper, if lamb was brined). Heat the 2 tablespoons of vegetable oil in a large frying pan over medium/high–high heat. When hot, season the lamb racks well with salt and place them in the pan. Brown each side of the lamb for 3–5 minutes then add the cubed butter. Once foaming, spoon the butter over the lamb racks until they are a deep golden colour. Transfer the racks to a roasting dish, pouring over the pan juices, and bake in the oven for 12–15 minutes. Remove, cover with foil and leave to rest.

4. Slice the courgettes in half, lengthways and gently score diagonal lines across the flesh, creating a diamond effect. Heat some of the pan juices from the lamb over medium-high heat in the same large frying pan you used to brown the lamb. Add the olive oil. Season the courgettes then place them, flesh side down, in the hot pan. Brown for 3–5 minutes, then turn them over and cook for a further 3 minutes. You might have to do this in batches. Sprinkle the Parmesan on the top of the courgettes.

5. To serve, carve the rested lamb racks from the back of the rack, between the bones. Serve 3 cutlets per person with the ragu and the courgettes, and torn basil leaves on top.

Lamb Hotpot

SERVES: 4 | PREP TIME: 25 MINUTES | COOKING TIME: 1 HOUR 35 MINUTES

Lancashire hotpot is a traditional dish from where I grew up in Southport. I think all of my books have a lamb hotpot of some form in them. This is a variation on the classic, so I will probably get a few comments from the Northerners! It is a dish that, done well, can take a little time, hence why it is in this chapter, but it's a one-stop meal, so is the sort of thing you can put in your oven in the morning and it's ready in the evening. It is traditionally served with pickled red cabbage, but I prefer it with green vegetables and some sourdough on the side to mop up all the sauce. Job done.

4 tbsp vegetable oil

2 onions, sliced

2 garlic cloves, finely grated

2 tbsp tomato purée

½ tsp cumin seeds

100ml red wine

750ml good-quality chicken or vegetable stock

4 tbsp Worcestershire sauce

1 tsp black treacle

2 bay leaves

¼ bunch of rosemary

¼ bunch of thyme

200g button mushrooms, quartered

4 tbsp plain flour

1 tsp ground white pepper

4 lamb neck fillets (about 150g each), cut into 1cm-thick slices

3 large potatoes (Desiree or King Edward), peeled and cut into 3mm-thick slices

50g butter, melted

sea salt

MARCUS' TIP:
Try making this with all-butter shortcrust or puff pastry instead of potatoes for a tasty lamb pie. Then serve with creamy mashed potatoes and sauerkraut.

1. Heat 2 tablespoons of the oil in a large saucepan over medium heat. Add half the onions, season with salt and cook for 10–15 minutes until golden, stirring frequently. Add the garlic, tomato purée and cumin seeds and cook for a few minutes. Add the wine and let it reduce to a syrup, then add the stock (reserving 4 tablespoons for the potatoes), Worcestershire sauce, treacle, bay leaves, rosemary and thyme to the pan. Cover and simmer gently for 30 minutes. Strain, season with salt and set aside.

2. Preheat the oven to 170°C/150°C fan/gas 4.

3. Heat 1 tablespoon of the vegetable oil in a large frying pan over high heat. Add the mushrooms, seasoning well with salt. Cook for about 10 minutes, until golden and the liquid has evaporated. Remove from the pan and set aside. Wipe the pan clean.

4. Heat the remaining tablespoon of oil in the large frying pan. When hot, add the remaining onion, and season well with salt. Cook over low-medium heat for 25–30 minutes until golden and caramelised, stirring frequently.

5. Season the flour with salt and the white pepper. Coat the slices of lamb in the seasoned flour and place a layer of the slices in a casserole dish. Add a layer of mushrooms, then a layer of onions. Top with the strained stock. Repeat with the remaining lamb, mushrooms and onions.

6. Mix the potato slices with the melted butter and reserved stock then layer them over the hot-pot mix in a spiral shape, covering the meat and sauce.

7. Set the casserole dish in a roasting tray to catch any sauce that bubbles over. Bake in the oven, uncovered, for 40 minutes until the lamb is just cooked through, then if needed, place under a hot grill for about 5 minutes to brown the top of the potatoes. Allow to rest for a few minutes then serve immediately.

'Nduja-stuffed Pork with Smoked Bacon and Red Wine Sauce

**SERVES: 6 | PREP TIME: 30 MINUTES, PLUS COOLING AND CHILLING
COOKING TIME: ABOUT 1 HOUR 20 MINUTES**

'Nduja (pronounced 'n-doo-ya') is a spicy, spreadable pork salami. It has a similar flavour profile to chorizo, but a bit more of a chilli kick. You can buy it fresh, or in a jar, with the former being preferable in flavour terms. It is used here to stuff the pork loin, so all the spicy flavour imparts into the loin. The red wine sauce adds a lovely acidity to the finished dish. I like to serve this with wilted greens and new potatoes.

FOR THE STUFFED PORK

45g butter
1 onion, finely diced
100g 'nduja, skin removed and roughly chopped (if using fresh)
100g fresh breadcrumbs
4 tbsp finely chopped flat-leaf parsley
50g whole toasted blanched almonds, roughly chopped (see page 126 for method)
2 large pork tenderloins, or fillets (900–1kg in total) (brined for 2 hours if you wish – use 1 quantity of the brine on page 242)
1 tbsp vegetable oil
sea salt and freshly ground black pepper

1. Heat 25g of the butter in a medium frying pan over medium heat. When melted, add the onion and cook for about 10 minutes, until soft. Add the 'nduja, turn down the heat and cook gently for about 10 minutes until some of the oil seeps out of the meat, then transfer to a glass or metal bowl (it will stain plastic). Add the breadcrumbs, parsley and almonds and mix well until combined. Cover and refrigerate.

2. Bring the pork chop to room temperature (rinsing off the brine and patting dry with kitchen paper, if pork was brined). Carefully cut down the length of the pork loins, halfway to the centre. Cover your chopping board with clingfilm and place a pork loin on top. Open it out where it has been sliced, cover with another layer of clingfilm then, using a rolling pin, flatten the pork to a thickness of 5mm. Repeat with the second fillet or loin.

3. Pat half of the stuffing mixture onto each piece of pork, leaving an edge on one long side of each fillet of 3cm. Roll each loin up tightly, starting at the long edge with the stuffing. Tie the pork tightly with kitchen string at a number of intervals across the rolled fillet/loin. Roll each loin tightly in clingfilm. Refrigerate them while you make the sauce.

4. To make the sauce, heat the vegetable oil in a medium saucepan over medium heat. When hot, add the shallots, carrot, celery, garlic and peppercorns. Cook for about 15 minutes, until golden, stirring frequently, then add the wine. Simmer for 10–15 minutes until the wine has reduced to a syrup, then add the beef stock, thyme and bay leaves. Simmer for 20 minutes then strain and return to a clean saucepan. In a small bowl, mix the cornflour with 2 tablespoons of water and whisk this into the sauce to thicken.

5. Preheat the oven to 230°C/210°C fan/gas 8.

FOR THE RED WINE SAUCE

2 tbsp vegetable oil
6 shallots, peeled and thickly sliced
1 carrot, peeled and cut into 5mm-thick slices
1 celery stick, cut into 5mm-thick slices
2 garlic cloves, halved
6 white peppercorns
250ml red wine
600ml good-quality beef stock
¼ bunch of thyme
2 bay leaves
3 tsp cornflour

6. Pour the oil for the pork into a roasting dish large enough for the stuffed pork and heat in the oven for 10 minutes.

7. Take the pork fillets out of the fridge and remove the clingfilm. Season with salt and pepper then carefully place into the preheated roasting dish. Roast for 8 minutes, turning them after 4 minutes, then reduce the heat to 200°C/180°C fan/gas 6 and add the remaining 20g butter to the roasting dish. Cook for a further 20–25 minutes, turning the pork every 5 minutes to make sure it's evenly browned.

8. Remove from the oven, cover with foil and rest for 10 minutes.

9. Remove the string from the pork, cut it into 2cm-thick slices (3–4 per serving) and serve with the sauce and accompaniments of your choice.

Port-braised Feather Blade Steaks with Potato, Onion and Horseradish Gratin

SERVES: 4 | PREP TIME: 30 MINUTES | COOKING TIME: ABOUT 5 HOURS

Also known as feather steak, this cut of meat is taken from the shoulder blade of the cattle. It has a feather-like connective tissue running through it, hence its name. When slowly braised it takes on a wonderful, slightly flaky texture. It needs to be cooked long and slow for optimum results, so do plan ahead. As you will need a much hotter oven for the gratin, I suggest cooking the steaks first. You can leave them to sit for an hour or two while you bake the gratin – just heat them up prior to serving.

2 tbsp vegetable oil

4 feather blade steaks (about 200g each)

1 onion, halved

4 garlic cloves, lightly bashed

2 carrots, halved crossways

1 leek, white part only, halved crossways

1 bunch of thyme

2 bay leaves

4 star anise

6 white peppercorns

2 tbsp tomato purée

300ml port

1½ litres good-quality beef stock

sea salt and freshly ground black pepper

1. Preheat the oven to 140°C/120°C fan/gas 1.

2. Start with the feather blade steaks. Heat the oil in a large, wide ovenproof saucepan or casserole dish over medium heat. Once hot, season the feather blade steaks with salt, then brown them, in batches, for about 5 minutes per batch, turning them halfway through. Transfer to a plate.

3. Add the onion, garlic, carrots, leek, half of the thyme, bay leaves, star anise and peppercorns to the pan or casserole dish and fry for 10–15 minutes until all the vegetables are lightly caramelised. Add the tomato purée and port and simmer for 15 minutes until the port has reduced to a syrup, then add 1.2 litres of the beef stock and bring to a very gentle simmer. Return the steaks and their resting juices to the pan, cover and carefully place in the oven to cook for 3 hours.

4. During the last hour, start preparing the gratin. Heat the vegetable oil and 25g of the melted butter in a large frying pan over medium heat. When hot, add the sliced onions and season well with salt and pepper. Cook for about 30 minutes, until golden, stirring frequently. While the onions are cooking, put the remaining 300ml beef stock and a quarter of the remaining thyme from above in a saucepan and bring to the boil. Cook for 2 minutes, then turn off the heat and leave to steep for 10 minutes before straining into a clean pan. Keep warm.

MARCUS' TIP:

Braised meats are perfect comfort food in the colder months. Meats with a higher fat content, such as pork belly or lamb breast. will result in a richer texture. Braised meats also freeze very well, so it's worth cooking a little extra to enjoy for a quick supper when you are tighter on prep time.

FOR THE POTATO, ONION AND HORSERADISH GRATIN

2 tbsp vegetable oil

100g butter, melted

3 onions, thinly sliced

4 large King Edward or Maris Piper
  potatoes (about 900g), peeled and cut
  into 3mm-thick slices

4 tbsp horseradish sauce

5. When the steaks are done, carefully remove them from the pan. Turn up the oven temperature to 200°C/180°C fan/gas 6. Strain the sauce from the steak pan into a clean pan and bring to a rapid boil. Reduce the sauce by half. Place the steaks back into the casserole dish and cover with a lid to keep warm while the sauce is reducing. Check the seasoning.

6. Place the potato slices for the gratin in a large bowl. Pick the leaves of the remaining thyme and add them to the potatoes. Add the remaining 75g of melted butter and season well. Mix with your hands to combine.

7. When the onions are ready, stir in the horseradish sauce. Layer one third of the potatoes in an ovenproof baking dish (about 20cm square). Top with half of the onions and one third of the thyme-infused beef stock. Repeat. Finish the gratin with the last of the potatoes and stock. Cover with foil and bake in the oven for 45 minutes. Remove the foil and bake for a further 25–30 minutes until golden.

8. To serve, pour the reduced sauce over the steaks in the casserole dish and cover with a lid. Bring to a simmer over low heat. Serve the warm steaks with the sauce and the gratin and wilted seasonal greens.

TARTS

Whether you make one large one or several individual ones, tarts are the perfect make-ahead dessert to end a dinner party. Here are two delicious recipes to try.

Milk Chocolate, Raspberry and Thyme Tart

SERVES: 8 | PREP TIME: 30 MINUTES, PLUS CHILLING AND COOLING | COOKING TIME: 1¼ HOURS

My favourite chocolate is milk, especially when it is cold from the fridge! This dessert is a rich and decadent dish, and very delicious. The raspberry and thyme cut through the sweetness of the chocolate and add something a little different. I suggest serving this with a thick crème fraîche, as it adds a creamy acidity which complements the tart very well.

FOR THE PASTRY

140g plain flour, plus extra for dusting
pinch of sea salt
90g cold butter, cubed
40g caster sugar
1 egg, beaten, plus 1 egg yolk

FOR THE CHOCOLATE, RASPBERRY AND THYME FILLING

300ml double cream
100ml milk
½ bunch of thyme
400g milk chocolate, broken into pieces or roughly chopped
3 eggs
10g freeze-dried raspberry pieces
1 tsp cocoa powder, to serve

1. To make the pastry, rub together the flour, sea salt and cold butter in a bowl until the mixture resembles breadcrumbs (or blitz in a food processor). Stir in the sugar and gradually add the beaten egg to form a soft, pliable dough (you might not need all the egg). Gently form the pastry into a ball, flatten it, then wrap it in clingfilm and chill for 30 minutes.

2. Dust a work surface lightly with flour, unwrap the pastry and roll it out to a 4mm-thick circle. Use it to line a 21–2cm, high-sided, loose-bottomed tart tin, leaving a little excess pastry to hang over the edges. Return to the fridge for 20 minutes.

3. Meanwhile, preheat the oven to 220°C/200°C fan/gas 7.

4. Line the pastry case with baking parchment and fill with baking beans. Sit the tart case on a baking sheet and bake in the oven for 10 minutes. Reduce the oven temperature to 180°C/160°C fan/gas 4 and bake the tart case for a further 15 minutes, until it starts to turn golden and becomes firm. Remove the baking beans and parchment, brush with the egg yolk and return the case to the oven for a further 5 minutes, until evenly golden.

RECIPE CONTINUES OVER THE PAGE

5. While the tart case is baking, start making the filling. Put the double cream, milk and thyme in a medium saucepan, bring to a simmer and let it simmer for 5 minutes. Remove from the heat, cover and set aside to infuse for 20 minutes. Strain into a clean saucepan, discarding the thyme and bring back to a simmer.

6. Place the chocolate in a heatproof bowl and pour the hot cream and milk over the top. Cover and leave to sit for 5 minutes. Add the eggs and, using a stick blender, mix until well combined. Pass through a fine sieve into a jug.

7. Reduce the oven temperature to 140°C/120°C fan/gas 1. Remove the oven tray slightly from the oven. With the tart case in the oven, pour the chocolate mix into the shell. Sprinkle the raspberry pieces on top and, using a spoon, swirl to distribute evenly.

8. Bake the tart for 40–45 minutes until there is just a slight wobble in the middle. Carefully remove from the oven and leave to cool. When cool enough to handle, trim away the excess pastry with a sharp knife, and when fully cool remove the tart from the tin.

9. To serve, dust with the cocoa powder and slice using a hot knife.

Fig and Hazelnut Tarts with Smoky Crème Fraîche

MAKES: 4 SMALL TARTS, OR 1 MEDIUM TART | PREP TIME: 30 MINUTES, PLUS CHILLING AND COOLING | COOKING TIME: UP TO 1 HOUR 10 MINUTES

These tarts are a variation on a type of Bakewell tart, but using hazelnuts and figs. They are glazed with smoky, rich, black lapsang souchong tea, which is also used to flavour the crème fraîche. This is a slightly more savoury pudding, so a great finish to a lighter meal.

FOR THE PASTRY
130g plain flour, plus extra for dusting
pinch of sea salt
85g cold butter, cubed
35g caster sugar
1 egg yolk

1. To make the pastry, rub together the flour, salt, cold butter and sugar in a bowl (or blitz in a food processor) until the mixture resembles breadcrumbs. Add the egg yolk and mix to form a soft, pliable dough. Wrap the dough in clingfilm and chill for 30 minutes.

2. Dust a work surface lightly with flour, unwrap the pastry and roll it out to 3mm thickness, then use it to line 4 × 10cm loose-bottomed tart tins, or 1 × 20cm loose-bottomed tart tin, leaving a little excess pastry to hang over the edges. Return the lined tin(s) to the fridge for 20 minutes.

FOR THE HAZELNUT FRANGIPANE

100g caster sugar

100g soft butter

2 eggs

pinch of sea salt

100g ground hazelnuts

5 tsp fig jam or apricot jam

6 large or 8 small ripe figs, each sliced
    into 8

FOR THE GLAZE AND CREAM

2 tsp lapsang souchong tea leaves or 1 tea
    bag

2 tbsp Frangelico

80g crème fraîche

MARCUS' TIP:

Pastry can be a fickle thing
to make and roll but the key is
ensuring you rest it long enough in
between each step – making, rolling,
trimming – and keep it cool enough. If
you are trying to roll pastry in a hot
kitchen, roll it bit by bit, putting it
back in the fridge frequently to
cool and firm up.

3. Meanwhile, preheat the oven to 220°C/200°C fan/gas 7.

4. Line the pastry case(s) with baking parchment and fill with baking beans. Sit the tart case(s) on a baking sheet and bake for 5 minutes. Reduce the oven temperature to 190°C/170°C fan/gas 5 and bake the tart case(s) for a further 10 minutes, until they start to turn golden. Remove the baking beans and parchment, and return the case to the oven for a further 5 minutes, until evenly golden. Remove from the oven and allow to cool slightly. When cool enough to handle, trim away the excess pastry with a sharp knife.

5. To make the frangipane, beat together the sugar and butter in a bowl until light and creamy. Add the eggs one at a time, beating well after each addition. Finally, mix in the pinch of salt and hazelnuts. Spread 1 teaspoon (or 1 tablespoon plus 1 teaspoon if making a large tart) of the jam on the bottom of each pastry case followed by the frangipane, then arrange the sliced figs on top, in a circular formation, slightly overlapping, to cover the whole tart. Bake the small tarts for 20–25 minutes or the medium tart for 50–60 minutes, until deep golden and the frangipane has just set in the centre. If the medium tart starts to brown before the cooking time, cover it loosely with foil for the remaining time. Remove from the oven and leave to cool on a wire rack for at least 15 minutes.

6. While the tart(s) cool, bring 100ml water to the boil then add the tea leaves or tea bag. Remove from the heat and allow to infuse for 6 minutes then strain. Place three quarters of the liquid into a small clean saucepan, bring to the boil and reduce by half, then place in the fridge to cool.

7. Mix the remaining quarter of tea with the remaining teaspoon of jam and 1 tablespoon of Frangelico in a small bowl. Liberally brush the top of the tart(s) with this syrup (you might have some left over). Leave to cool a little in the tins before removing and serving.

8. Place the crème fraîche in a bowl and add the cooled tea and remaining Frangelico. Whisk together until slightly stiff. Serve with the tarts.

Burnt Honey Parfait with White Chocolate and Apricot

**SERVES: 4 | PREP TIME: 25 MINUTES, PLUS CHILLING AND COOLING
COOKING TIME: ABOUT 25 MINUTES**

I had an excess of honey this year from the hives on the farm so this was a delicious way to use some of it. Caramelising the honey reduces the sweetness and adds a more savoury, smoky flavour, without sacrificing its fragrance. This dish is a perfect summer pudding, when apricots are at their best.

50g dried apricots, sliced

3 tbsp honey

2 large ripe apricots

25ml apricot liqueur, peach schnapps or amaretto

FOR THE PARFAIT

150g honey

2 leaves of gelatine

4 egg yolks

300ml double cream

100g white chocolate, broken into pieces

1. Put the honey for the parfait in a small saucepan and bring to the boil. Meanwhile, soak the gelatine in a shallow bowl of cold water for 5 minutes to soften, and line a 1-litre square or rectangular plastic container with baking parchment.

2. Put the egg yolks in a heatproof bowl and set the bowl over a pan of gently simmering water (making sure the bowl does not touch the water). When the honey has turned a dark golden colour – this will take 5–7 minutes – pour it over the yolks and beat with an electric whisk for 7–9 minutes until you have a really thick and creamy mixture that holds ribbon shapes when the whisk is lifted. Squeeze the water from the gelatine and drop one sheet at a time into the mixture, whisking as it dissolves.

3. Remove the bowl from the heat and continue to whisk for up to 10 minutes until the mixture has cooled.

4. Whisk the double cream in a bowl until it forms soft peaks. Fold the whipped cream into the egg mixture until smooth. Transfer to the lined container and put in the freezer for at least 3 hours.

5. Take the parfait out of the freezer and remove it from the container, peeling the baking parchment off. Cut the parfait into 4 even rectangles and place these back in the freezer.

6. Cut 4 rectangles of baking parchment that will fit around each parfait, with a 1cm overhang on the shortest side.

7. Melt the white chocolate in a heatproof bowl over a pan of gently simmering water. Lay each parchment rectangle on your bench and cover them in the melted white chocolate. Take one parfait at a time and place at one end of the chocolate. Using a knife or your hands, gently roll the parfait up in the parchment, as tight as you can, then place in the freezer immediately.

8. Place the dried apricots in a small saucepan and cover with hot water. Place over the heat and simmer gently for 10 minutes. Remove from the heat and allow to cool slightly, then drain. Put the apricots in a blender with 2 tablespoons of the honey and blitz until smooth, adding a tablespoon of water if needed to loosen the purée. Pass through a fine sieve.

9. Cut the fresh, ripe apricots in half and remove the stones. Cut each half into 4 segments. Place in a shallow dish and cover with 1 tablespoon of honey and the liqueur.

10. To serve, spoon the dried apricot purée onto each plate. Take the parfaits out of the freezer, remove the parchment and place one on each plate. Finish by placing the apricot segments on and around the parfaits.

Pear and Star Anise Tarte Tatin
with Buttermilk Ice Cream

SERVES: 4–6 | PREP TIME: 25 MINUTES, PLUS FREEZING
COOKING TIME: ABOUT 1 HOUR

This is one of the best desserts to come out of France. Whether it's made with pear, apple or banana, a tarte Tatin just cannot be beaten. It's got to be oozing with fruit, oozing with caramel, it's got to be piping hot and it's got to have crunchy puff pastry. It takes some practice, but is very, very satisfying when you get it right. For this recipe, I suggest using Conference pears, as they are a little firmer and drier than other varieties – even so, I recommend drying them out for 3 days.

FOR THE TARTE TATIN

5–6 large or 8 small Conference pears
100g cold butter
1 x 320g sheet of ready-rolled all-butter
   puff pastry
100g caster sugar
2 star anise

FOR THE BUTTERMILK ICE
CREAM

280ml cultured buttermilk
50ml milk
280ml double cream
2 tbsp runny honey
200g condensed milk

1. Peel, quarter and core the pears and leave them in the fridge for 3 days, so they dry out a little.

2. Make the ice cream before baking the tarte tatin so it can freeze while you bake. Put the buttermilk, milk, double cream, honey and condensed milk in a large bowl. Blend using a stick blender until smooth. Strain the mix through a fine sieve into a metal or plastic freezerproof container. Cover and freeze for about 1½ hours, until the base and sides are starting to freeze. Remove from the freezer and vigorously stir with a balloon whisk (or an electric whisk) until smooth. Refreeze, then repeat 3 or 4 more times at hourly intervals so that you end up with a smooth, creamy ice cream. If you have an ice-cream machine, follow the manufacturer's instructions and you should have softly frozen ice cream within about 20 minutes.

3. Preheat the oven to 190°C/170°C fan/gas 5. Remove the butter from the fridge to allow it to soften slightly. Unroll the puff pastry sheet and cut it into a 24cm diameter circle (the same size or a little larger than the top diameter of the frying pan you use in the next step). Place back on its baking parchment and refrigerate.

4. Squash the slightly softened butter into a 20cm diameter (at the base) ovenproof pan. Ensure there is an even layer on the base then add the sugar and swirl the pan to distribute evenly.

5. Grate the star anise into the sugar. Place the first piece of pear into the sugared butter, with the base at the edge of the pan, tip pointing towards the middle, then lay the rest of the pear pieces in the pan, covering each other like fallen dominoes, placing them around the outer part of pan.

MARCUS' TIP:
You can make the whole thing a day ahead – just don't turn it out of the pan until you're ready to serve: heat it up on the hob, get the caramel loose again, put it into the oven briefly to warm it up, then it will be just as good as if you'd cooked it that day.

6. Place the pan over medium-high heat for about 10 minutes, until the butter and sugar begin to bubble and a golden caramel begins to form, then remove the pastry from the fridge and place it on top of the pears. Bake in the oven for about 45 minutes, until the pastry is cooked through and golden. Remove from the oven and allow to rest for 5–7 minutes before placing a plate on top of the pan then flipping the entire pan over, whereby the tarte tatin should slip gracefully onto the plate, ready to be sliced. Serve with the buttermilk ice cream.

Index

Acknowledgements

I am delighted with this book. It started as a discussion about my family's new kitchen garden in Sussex and has resulted in a relaxed, honest and beautiful record of seasonal recipes for the whole year. I am hugely proud of the book and have a great team, who worked so well together, to thank.

From day one Katya Shipster, my new editor, embraced my excitement about produce, our Sussex garden, cooking with seasonal ingredients and the journey from garden to plate. She allowed the ideas to flow and gently channelled them into a format that I hope you will enjoy. Thank you – I am delighted with the result.

Chantelle Nicholson, a hugely talented and successful chef, restaurateur and food author in her own right, has been my co-author for the sixth time. Thank you, CN – I hope you know that I couldn't do it without you, and I still have no idea how you fit everything into your day.

Photographer Susan Bell has been a very welcome new addition to the team. Clearly a perfectionist, she never stops until she gets the exact shot she is looking for, yet without pressure or stress. Thank you, Susan – I am so impressed by your work ethic and the many beautiful images that bring the recipes, and my garden, to life. Thanks also to your assistants, Facundo Bustamante and Maria Aversa.

James Empringham, art director, is always a massive pleasure to work with. Your easy manner makes the whole experience relaxed and enjoyable and automatically gets the best from us all. Thank you – this is our third book together and I just love it.

Becks Wilkinson did an amazing job on the food styling front. I was so impressed – the dishes you see in the book really did taste as good as they look and this is all down to Becks and her assistants in the kitchen, Dominique Eloise and Jo Jackson.

Tabitha Hawkins' prop styling was the final piece of the jigsaw – thank you for your creativity, your eye for the perfect setting and your energy.

Chefs are not always natural writers or sharers of information, so project editor Sarah Hammond is essential in the book process, ensuring that everything works as it should for the reader and nothing is missed out. Thanks also to copy editor Laura Nickoll and recipe tester Jenna Leiter – both vitally important.

Calm, methodical and very knowledgeable, Anatoliy Onischenko has been the voice of reason in our kitchen garden in Sussex for two years now. I continue to learn from him and have huge respect for what he does and how he goes about it. Observing Anatoliy as he manages our bee hives is wonderful to watch. Thank you for your patience.

I must also thank Rosemary Scoular at United Agents; Josie Turner, Jasmine Gordon, Tom Dunstan, Alice Gomer and Anna Derkacz from HarperCollins; and, of course, my restaurant teams who do such a great job and allow me the time to do this.

Finally, I would like to thank my family – Jane, Jake, Archie, Jessie and of course Esme the cocker spaniel. They all appear in this book, three years since their last appearance in *Marcus at Home*. It's amazing to see how much our children have changed in such a short space of time. Thank you for your love and support, guys. Remember, I do it all for you!